# STORIES
# I LOVE
# TO
# TELL

# OTHER BOOKS BY GENE EDWARDS

*The Divine Romance*

*A Tale of Three Kings*

*The Prisoner in the Third Cell*

*The Chronicles of Heaven (five volumes)*

*The First-Century Diaries (five volumes)*

*The Day I Was Crucified*

*The Story of My Life as Told by Jesus Christ*

# STORIES
# I LOVE
# TO
# TELL

## GENE
## EDWARDS

## EMANATE
### BOOKS

Published in Nashville, Tennessee, by Emanate Books, an imprint of Thomas Nelson. Nelson Books and Thomas Nelson are registered trademarks of HarperCollins Christian Publishing, Inc.

Thomas Nelson titles may be purchased in bulk for educational, business, fund-raising, or sales promotional use. For information, please e-mail SpecialMarkets@ThomasNelson.com.

Any Internet addresses, phone numbers, or company or product information printed in this book are offered as a resource and are not intended in any way to be or to imply an endorsement by Thomas Nelson, nor does Thomas Nelson vouch for the existence, content, or services of these sites, phone numbers, companies, or products beyond the life of this book.

ISBN 978-0-7852-1869-2 (HC)
ISBN 978-0-7852-1874-6 (eBook)

Library of Congress Control Number: 2017956695

Printed in the United States of America
18 19 20 21 22  LSC  10 9 8 7 6 5 4 3 2 1

# DEDICATION

*We all think highly of our family physicians. My family physician is extraordinary. He did not end his medical knowledge with earning his MD, but began with it. He spends a good part of every day learning all the fields of the healing arts. For every condition or disease he seems to have a half-dozen ways of treating the malady. I consider him to be perhaps the best physician among the finest. It is unlikely I would be alive today except for his applying the best of medical knowledge as known by internal medicine specialists plus alternative approaches which aid the healing process. With profound appreciation to my doctor, Stephen Grable, MD*

# CONTENTS

# CONTENTS

# INTRODUCTION

I learned early in my childhood that storytelling is a unique and often oblique way of making a point. Long before the invention of the microscope, the writer of Proverbs predicted that someday there would be discovered secrets in the snow that none had ever imagined. I hope that as you read these stories, you will discover secrets that the Holy Spirit gives to you exclusively.

# CHAPTER 1

# POOR WHITE TRASH

There are, in every generation, men who are admired for their simple upbringing of being born and raised in a log cabin; two such people were Abraham Lincoln and Andrew Jackson. But then there are those who could tell a story that would make being raised in a log cabin look like paradise.

Gladys did not grow up in a log cabin, or even in a dugout. Gladys grew up in a storm cellar, which is essentially a hole in the ground to climb into when a tornado is approaching. It usually goes down into the ground about six feet and is usually about six feet wide and six feet long. Some have concrete or wood walls; others are simply the dirt itself. Gladys knew storm cellars as her home. In fact, the words "poor white trash" were often used in reference to her parents, her sisters and brothers, and herself. The term was coined before the Civil War and was simply meant as a reference to white people who were living on the same level as the slaves. The term persisted after the Civil War and the emancipation of the slaves. It still had the same meaning: whites living on the same level as the poorest of all the people in our nation. It was a term used for the strata of human society that she would break from.

The story of Gladys's fight to leave the chains of poor white trash is as heroic as any tale you will ever hear.

Mr. Brewer, Gladys's father, had a terrible phobia of tornadoes. He felt certain that one day he was going to be sucked up into one of them, so he confined his entire family to living in storm cellars. He was also an alcoholic. The way the family made a living was to follow the local cotton fields of Oklahoma during the five months of the cotton-picking harvest. Each one of the children was to pick one dollar's worth of cotton per day. It was an almost impossible task, but nonetheless it was the expected lot.

Gladys understood that the way out of the life she was living was to get a high school education, something which no one in her family tree had ever accomplished. The possibility of actually graduating from high school seemed beyond reach. Five months of the year Gladys was in the cotton fields of Oklahoma, and the rest of the year her parents and other three siblings did whatever they could to earn some money. The great question in her life was, how many miles are there between the cotton fields—where she was on her knees picking cotton all day—and the nearest grammar school? Getting to that school and managing to receive a full year's education simply seemed impossible.

This is what Gladys's life looked like.

Her father and mother had managed to put up six beds in the storm cellar that they borrowed and lived in. The cotton sack that held the cotton she picked every day was her mattress. Inside that cotton sack were two things: a paper sack, which held the totality of all her clothes, and her books.

On days when it was raining hard, there were no

workers in the cotton fields. Gladys would rise long before daybreak and walk to the school. It was not unusual for the first person to open the schoolhouse door to find Gladys sleeping in the doorway. There she would ask her teacher for the assignments for the week. She begged for damaged copies of the books so that she could draw from them for the coming week. She did her schoolwork at night by candlelight, not in the storm cellar but on the ground above it. Gladys was an A student.

Gladys would have her teachers check the work she had done and then return to the cotton field to pick cotton late into the night until she knew she had picked enough cotton to reach the standard of one dollar's worth per day. When the teachers of the school began to understand who Gladys was, they gave her books to read and gave her special work and assignments to study for the coming year.

In good weather, she slept on her cotton sack waiting for the cotton to be weighed, not at the end of the day but at dawn of a new day. If there were light showers during the night, Gladys would simply take shelter inside the ten-foot-long canvas cotton cover that was part of her life.

Food came from the legendary side-of-the-road grocery store and gas station. It was the custom of some of
those cotton-field owners to allow the poor white trash
to come in and use the stove for a few hours when the
stove was not being used.

On some of these vast cotton fields, the owners had
erected something which could only be called the shell
of a house. There was a roof and walls, nothing else.
There were door frames but no doors; window frames
but no windows; rafters of the attic rather than ceilings;
four rooms but no kitchen and no furniture. Nearby
was an outhouse and a dug water well along with the
faithful water pump everyone was free to use.

Bathing was something that took place at night
when there was no more work to be done. Her sister
would pump the water while Gladys soaped herself all
over, if soap was available. Her sister made sure that
there would be no males anywhere nearby. At times, the
owners of the fields showed Gladys grace and favor, and
she might be allowed to use a tub that would be placed
in the backyard and filled with water. This was the only
known bathtub for blacks, whites, and even the owners
of the field. A bathtub would allow you to actually take

a bath, which was a luxury out in the burning hot plains of Oklahoma.

Oklahoma was well known for droughts that often lasted one, two, or three years. Although cotton is a hot weather crop, needing little water, still there were years so severe that virtually no cotton grew. Those were the times when Gladys could actually sit in the classroom.

On Sundays, it mattered not the name of the church, Gladys was in church. Sometimes, because of her bare feet and tattered clothes, she would sit in the foyer or slip into a back row and flee during the closing prayer. She later said, "I always drew strength from a scripture, a sermon, or songs, to inspire me to believe maybe it can be done!"

At the age of nine Gladys owned her first pair of shoes, secondhand shoes given to her by one of the gracious owners of a cotton field.

In her seventeenth year, one of the drought years, Gladys graduated from high school. The faculty provided her with a new dress and a pair of shoes. When she was given her diploma, she received a standing ovation, but she received something more than that on that hallowed day.

In those days, when a high school education was so rare, Gladys could now teach kindergarten and the first, second, and third grades. But Gladys had several dreams and steadfast goals. One of them was to get a year's education in college, which would allow her to teach grammar school. With nothing but the paper sack that contained her few meager clothes, she moved to a town with a college in it. She attended night school whenever there were classes that fulfilled the curriculum for her first year of education. Gladys had no private room, but she did work out arrangements with a family to sleep at night on their sofa in exchange for taking care of the housekeeping and caring for children six days a week. She found enough odd jobs to pay for food.

One of the jobs that Gladys had on Saturdays was working at a cleaners. One Saturday a young man came in to have his suit cleaned. He was medium height, dark, and handsome. She put a note into his suit's lapel pocket with only two words, "Hi, handsome." It is said he cut quite a stride because he was built like a Greek god. They soon married.

Gladys finished her first year of college. Now she could begin taking education courses and go through a

7

year of tutorial training under a certified teacher. Meanwhile, she was working as a part-time kindergarten teacher.

Gladys was married that same year at the age of nineteen, and she later became the mother of two boys. She now had another dream: to see her two sons graduate from college, something unprecedented, never even dreamed of, on either side of the children's family tree. Her hope was to have two children who would turn out to be boy geniuses. That dream was soon crushed to the ground.

Gladys's elder son spent three years in the first grade. The fourth year he was allowed into the second grade simply by mercy. Gladys took some hope when it was found that the reason he was failing was because he had one wandering eye. By having a patch placed over one eye for the next year, the two eyes came together. After that, the older son took a normal trek to high school until his junior year, when he dropped out of school to join the army.

There was no such luck for the younger boy. He was the bane of Gladys's existence. There was no question that this child, at best, had come up short in learning skills. No one could read his handwriting, including the boy himself.

Math was a wonderland that he could not understand beyond the third grade. There was not a single word he could spell correctly. At the end of every school year, his grades would be Ds and on occasion an F. But Gladys found a way around that. She was now a teacher in a one-room schoolhouse. She had students in the first through the sixth grades, no one in the seventh grade, and three students in their last year of grammar school.

Gladys's solution was simple: she would take her pathetic son and enroll him in her one-room schoolhouse, tutoring him night and day. When she felt he might be able to handle that particular year, she would transfer her son back to the grammar school in town with a report card that showed he had passed the grade before. Unfortunately, the year he was in the seventh grade, there were no seventh-grade students; therefore her younger son had to go to school in town. He failed, and Gladys enrolled him in her eighth grade and ignored his report card. The son graduated from grammar school.

By this time, Gladys and her husband had a home. It

was tiny: twenty feet by twenty feet. The kitchen was so small it was difficult to even call it a kitchen. Everyone ate on a card table in the living room. There was only one bedroom, but there was indoor plumbing. In the living room was a chair and a sofa that could be pulled out as a bed at night. There was storage space underneath the sofa, which served as a place for the two boys' clothes.

But the other items under the sofa gave Gladys second thoughts about her younger son's intelligence. Somewhere between twenty and one hundred books lay under that sofa. They were the great classics of English literature. The younger son could read; at least, he could read until someone asked him to read out loud. He loved books and he would read anything. Gladys saved up enough money to buy a set of encyclopedias. Her younger son eventually read the entire set.

As Gladys wondered about this boy's intelligence, she drove him all the way to the state capital, walked into the place where IQ tests were given, and announced in a loud voice, "My son is either a moron or a genius, and I want you to find out which it is." Gladys, a blue-eyed Irish girl, had a very quick wit. When they handed her the results of the IQ test, the story goes, she looked at the results, looked up at the instructors who had administered the test, and asked, "Is this the IQ of my son or is it the IQ of the entire state of Texas?"

Still, the boy kept failing classes. Now old enough to understand what an IQ was, he drove to a college in another part of the state and asked to take an entrance exam. According to the way the story was told, he made the highest grade ever on that entrance exam. Six months later, he enrolled in college at the age of fifteen. In fact, he was the first person in his entire family tree to graduate from college. Gladys was present at his graduation, and one of her dreams had been fulfilled. Just a few weeks later, she graduated from college herself. The other son had returned from the army, went back to college, and he, too, graduated shortly after his mother.

Gladys had one other goal in life. She wanted to write a novel and see it published. That never happened. But everyone in her family and neighborhood remembers the day Gladys went down the street yelling, "I sold a short story. I sold a short story!" In one hand was the letter, and in the other hand was a $10 check for her short story entitled "The $100 Tip."

The boys grew up and both married. Gladys received her master's degree, the first one ever given in the field of dyslexia. She was the first person in the state certified to teach students with the learning handicap of dyslexia—not being able to spell or do math—but at that point she already had ten years' experience educating her own son. Eventually Gladys became one of the nation's leading authorities on dyslexia.

Gladys lived long enough to see her older son's four children grow up. They were each brilliant and each rose to the top of their professions—two lawyers and two judges. She did not live long enough to see her younger son's two daughters grow up. One daughter earned two master's degrees in education and management and the other became a college English teacher.

Gladys lived long enough to see her older son become superintendent of schools in the very educational system where he had failed the first grade three times. She also lived long enough to see the bane of her life, that "slow learner," become the author of more than two score books, which have been translated into some ninety-nine languages.

Word reached the younger son while he was on a

speaking tour in Europe that his mother was dying. He immediately returned to the United States, but not before he stopped by a publishing house where he received the first copy of the first edition of his third book. When he walked into his mother's room, he fell at her feet and began kissing her feet and covering them with tears.

He placed into her hand a church history book and then read the dedication page, which read:

This book is dedicated to GLADYS EDWARDS,
who, again and again, gave away all her substance
and lived out her whole life on this earth
for two who called her Mom.
She was my all-time number-one fan
and one of the dearest treasures
God in His merciful providence
ever bestowed on a son.
See you again, Mom,
in realms of blazing light
where none can be found except we be found in God.

Gladys *is* my mother.

# CHAPTER 2

# THE DAY I MET HELEN KELLER

Helen Keller was considered to be the most famous woman of not only the nineteenth century but also of the twentieth century. Her *story* has now been told for four generations. Movies have been made of her life. Anne Bancroft won an Academy Award for portraying the life of Miss Sullivan, who brought Helen Keller out of a world where there was neither sight nor sound. Patty Duke's portrayal of Helen Keller as a child will forever go down in Hollywood's legends as one of the greatest acting performances of all time.

It is one thing to meet one of the world's greatest and best-known people; it is another to meet them under the most unusual of circumstances. In fact, I'd say it is nothing less than momentous when you meet that person in one of the greatest moments of her life. It turned out also to be one of the most memorable moments of *my* life.

I was in Jerusalem. I was nineteen years old, and I had been living in the Holy Land. At this point, I was living in Jordan. I made it my habit to go as often as possible to a place called the Garden Tomb.

An English general had discovered this tomb, which many believe to be the place where Christ was buried and resurrected. The general's name was Gordon, and for a long time it was known as Gordon's Tomb. Later, under the loving care of Episcopalians, a gate was built in front of the tomb, and the place became known as it is today: the Garden Tomb.

One week earlier, many visitors had celebrated Easter there. Now it was time for me to leave the Holy Land to journey to Rome to study archaeology. I rose early in the morning, made my way through the streets of Jerusalem, and came to the gate of the Garden Tomb.

As soon as I walked through the gate, I realized that

two people had entered before me and were inside the tomb itself. After a while I began to realize that one was a woman, but the voice of the second person was a complete mystery to me. I had never heard a voice quite like it. It had no intonations; it was the flattest monotone I had ever heard. I then realized that whoever was in the tomb had a great deal to say.

Once through the narrow door of the tomb, I saw a hand stretched out toward heaven. Shortly afterward I discovered who was visiting in the tomb at that moment.

I had read about Helen Keller in seventh grade. I knew the story of her blindness and total loss of hearing. Helen had come from a wealthy family. Miss Sullivan, who herself had very low eyesight, was brought in to teach Helen how to understand handwriting in her own palm, giving her a way to make contact with the world around her. Something many people do not know is that Helen became proficient, not only understanding words written in her palm, but almost unbelievably, she learned how to speak. Her father invited his pastor to come to the Keller home to meet Helen and to lead her to a saving knowledge of Jesus Christ.

At the same time I was in Jerusalem, Helen Keller

was visiting there on a world tour to bring greater world consciousness to the plight of the blind.

Helen Keller, being led by a lady who had taken Miss Sullivan's place, was coming out of the tomb. I had not yet seen her face. The moment Helen stepped out of the tomb, I instantly recognized her. She stepped out of the tomb with her face turned toward the sky, one hand held in a gesture of praise, and a moment later both hands raised to heaven. At that very second, the morning sun broke over the wall of the Garden Tomb and shone directly on Helen Keller. I was transfixed. Then Miss Keller began to cry, tears pouring down her face. I was completely immobilized. Soon my tears joined with hers, and I raised my hands to the heavens too.

I had heard her say something in the tomb, and now she was saying it again in her strangely flat monotone voice that I could not fully understand. As she moved away from the tomb, her companion motioned for me to come over. I was about to actually meet Helen Keller!

While she was still crying and with her hands lifted to heaven, her companion took one hand and began to write in it: "There is someone who wants to meet you."

I spoke to her friend, telling her I was a young

minister, and said, "Thank you for giving me the privilege of sharing this moment with you."

She began again, and this time her words were very clear: *"There is no darkness here!"*

Over and over: "There is no darkness here! There is no darkness here!"

Helen had been in Jerusalem for several days. She had been to many churches that were dark, dim, and musty with incense. There was no circulating air. The darkness was engulfing.

She stood there transfixed, the sun falling on her face, her face sparkling with tears.

Without sound and without sight, Miss Keller had a keen relationship with the Christ *within*. She was never shy about testifying of Him.

She stood before that site of the resurrection, understanding better than any of us that in Christ there is no darkness at all.

Of all the memories I have turned to in my life, the one to which I return most frequently is the moment when Helen Keller, face aglow, stepped out of the resurrection tomb of the Lord, declaring the simple truth that in Christ there is no darkness.

# CHAPTER 3

# THE MIRACLE AT THE WAILING WALL

There is a story told of a Jewish father and his son who did not get along. There were many arguments between them, many statements spoken that both would later regret. The height of their clashing occurred when the young son came home one day and announced to his father that he had become a Christian. Furious, the father ordered the son to leave his home immediately: "You have never been born. You do not exist. I will never acknowledge that you were ever my son. You are completely disowned!"

The son did leave home. Years later the young man did something that many Hebrews choose to do, to return and visit the ancient Jewish homeland of Israel.

So it was that the young man made his way to the Holy Lands. Like so many tourists before him, he visited many of the sights with which you and I are familiar from the Old Testament. Being a Christian, he also visited areas where Jesus had walked and talked, and where other events of the church had taken place.

One site he visited was the ancient and venerated Wailing Wall.

More than two millennia ago, Solomon built the great temple, which was erected in Jerusalem. Solomon wanted there to be a vast courtyard surrounding the western side of the temple, but there was no land there. The temple had been built on a mound. Solomon ordered the building of a great retaining wall. The retaining wall was as high as the temple grounds; the stones were large and very strong. When this large retaining wall had been built, between it and the temple was a vast, unfilled gully. Slowly the area filled with soil and stone. When finished, there was a vast courtyard surrounding the temple. With the passing of the years, one might walk on the surface of that open courtyard never know-ing that it used to be a gully or that the retaining wall had been built in order to create the courtyard.

The young Christian man—disowned by his father—came to the wall. He then did exactly what so many hundreds of thousands of other Jews had done before him: he prayed.

In recent years, the Wailing Wall in Jerusalem had been under the control of the Jewish people. But for nearly two thousand years, Jerusalem was controlled by the Roman Empire and the Muslims. Yet, through most of those times, Jews had been able to come to this wall and pray for the liberation of Jerusalem. That prayer was not answered until the twentieth century.

Now the tradition persists. Devout Jews come to the Wailing Wall with their prayers to God. These devotees of God write their prayers on a small sheet of paper, roll it up tightly, and place it in the cracks of the wall.

On this particular occasion, the young man did something other than that.

First he asked the Lord to forgive him for the way he had treated his father when he was growing up. Then he asked if there was some way he and his father could find each other and that his father could forgive him. Very carefully, the young man wrote out his prayer and signed his name to it. He rolled up the small sheet of paper to place it in one of the cracks of the wall.

Now if you have ever been to the Wailing Wall, you know there are two sides to it. It is high, vast, and covered with thousands of cracks and crevices. On both the west and south sides on any given day you might see ten thousand sheets of paper, which have been placed into those cracks in the Wailing Wall. The young man reached up to place his written prayer in just such a crack. As he did so, he accidently dislodged another prayer, and it fell to the ground.

The young man reached down to pick up the dislodged sheet of paper. In so doing, he became curious, wondering what language the prayer that fell loose had been written in: perhaps in Hebrew, perhaps in Arabic, perhaps in some language he had never known or heard. He unrolled the sheet of paper, knowing that in a moment he would place it back into the wall.

As he read, the young man was stunned and then shaken. He immediately recognized the handwriting of his father! The note read, "Oh, God, I do not know where my son is. Forgive me for the way I mistreated him. Somehow bring us together. Let me have the courage to tell my Christian son that I, too, have received Jesus as the true Messiah."

Eventually the young man located his father. They embraced, they wept, they both forgave, and the two men became reconciled.

God's version of a coincidence.

# CHAPTER 4

# THANK GOD YOU GOT
# OFF THE PHONE

In a village about twenty miles from the nearest hospital, in the early part of the twentieth century, lived a young married couple. The husband was the minister of the small village. He and his wife had a child. At the time our story takes place, the minister had been delivering a series of messages on prayer.

It came about that the minister's son began to develop a cough. The cough became more serious, and suddenly the boy's throat closed up and he could not breathe. Panicked, the pastor called the hospital. Both he and the doctor who answered knew that the boy would be dead before help could arrive. The minister hung up the phone and began calling other places, asking, "Do you know of any doctor who is anywhere near our village?" The answer was always no, but the minister continued making his frantic phone calls. His son was near the point of death. He suddenly remembered what he had been preaching each Sunday morning. He stopped calling, and he prayed.

"Lord, please save my child. Please work a miracle and save his life. As hard as it is, if it is not Your will, thank You for giving us this precious boy. We yield to Your will. We accept Your will, whatever it is."

The phone rang, and the first words the minister heard were, "Thank God you got off the telephone! We have just discovered that there is a doctor visiting your village right now." But even with these miraculous words, the minister was keenly aware that unless the doctor arrived within the next few seconds, his son would be dead.

The voice on the other end of the telephone continued, "We don't know the exact location, but we do have the address of the house where the doctor is visiting."

The minister stopped to find a pen and paper to write down the address when he realized that the address he was hearing belonged to his neighbor next door.

Astounded, the minister took his son up into his arms, ran to the porch, threw open the door, and yelled one word: *"Tracheotomy!"* Within seconds, the doctor performed the tracheotomy.

The boy lived.

All this came to pass because a minister paused to recall what he had taught about prayer.

# CHAPTER 5

# A TALE OF TWO COINS

The Players, or the Players Club, is a private social club that was founded in New York City in the late nineteenth century. It began as a very small restaurant not too far from Broadway. On opening night, the actors ("players") would hang out in front of the restaurant until the morning newspaper arrived to see what the critics had written about their play. What the critics in New York City wrote about any play was usually either the doom or the success of the show. Eventually, the Players became an organization of actors that later enlarged itself to be an association of not only some of New York's most famous actors but also of the wealthiest people in New York City.

Once a group of men were dining at the Players Club. All the men at the table except one were members of that highly esteemed club. One man was a guest. While sitting there, the men told stories of the different influences in their lives.

One of the men told a most remarkable tale. Just that morning he had purchased one of the rarest coins in the world. The coin was famous, and there were only two ever struck. Their value was almost inestimable.

During the meal, the man passed the coin around for everyone to inspect. At the end of the meal, he asked that his coin be returned to him. No one had the coin, nor was there offered any explanation for its disappearance. The police were called in. All the men present volunteered to be searched by the police; that is, everyone except the guest. He adamantly refused to be searched. He was just as adamant that he had not stolen the coin. The restaurant put up screens around the entire area, and everyone was kept within the parameters of the screens.

In the meantime, a waiter was cleaning off the table, only to discover that the coin had somehow fallen into the flower pot in the center of the table.

Everyone, from the members of the club to the police, breathed a sigh of relief. Someone looked at the guest and asked him, "Why on earth did you refuse to be searched when you knew you would certainly look guilty?"

His response stunned everyone. The guest reached into his pocket, pulled out a coin, and displayed it in the palm of his hand. It was identical to the first coin. He held in his hand the only other coin of its kind in the world.

"I knew the coins had come on the market, just as you did. This morning you purchased one of those coins. I purchased the other one."

These two rare coins were both at that table at the same time.

I often retell this story to myself so that I will not make the kind of mistake that was made that day.

# CHAPTER 6

# A FAIRY-TALE WEDDING

He saw her across the room on Sunday morning. She was in the choir, and she had just become the secretary of the First Baptist Church in Commerce, Texas. She was so extraordinarily beautiful that it was love at first sight for him, but he doubted that she could ever be his because anyone of such loveliness simply was not going to be part of his life. Yet, after several years of courtship, she fell in love with him as well. They began to plan their wedding.

He wanted a very simple wedding, consisting of

nothing but the pastor, a witness, and the two of them exchanging vows. She, of course, had her heart set on a beautiful traditional wedding. They argued about it. Eventually there were tears, forgiveness, and compromise. The young man drove the young lady back to her home, which was in Fort Worth. Their eyes still tearstained, he pulled up in the driveway of the home where she was living with her mother and father. To their surprise, her mother was standing on the porch with a Western Union telegram in her hand. Once they spied the telegram they knew exactly what had happened and what was in that wire. Until that moment, they had forgotten that they had written their love story and sent it to NBC!

At that time, in the mid-1950s, there was a morning television program entitled *Bride and Groom*. NBC chose some lucky couple to be married on television in front of an estimated five million people. NBC received an average of one hundred applications per day, or five hundred letters per week, from couples seeking to be chosen.

The young couple had mailed in their love story and told how they had resolved their conflict of two separate callings.

The telegram read very simply, "We read your love story. NBC's *Bride and Groom* extends to you an invitation to be married on national television on May 13, 1954."

Well, all their wedding plans went out the window. The couple could not have conceived of anything so extraordinary.

Later they found out that there was a bit of a problem. At that time there were only three television channels: ABC, NBC, and CBS. Also, at that particular time, the McCarthy hearings were being covered on all three stations. No one would see the wedding. The usual five million people who watched *Bride and Groom* would all be watching the McCarthy hearings instead, no matter which channel they turned to.

The gentleman in charge of NBC for the state of Texas wrote a letter protesting that there was a young couple from Texas who was going to be married, and Texans wanted to see that wedding.

The day before the wedding at Studio B on the second floor of Rockefeller Plaza, they were informed that the people who turned on their televisions in Texas that morning would be able to view the wedding after all.

The people in charge surmised that the television viewers of America were very tired of the McCarthy hearings and there would be an awful lot of Texans who would tune in that day.

And so came the morning of the filming, and there was more wonderful news. The young groom had had the audacity to send a letter to the Reverand Dr. Frank Laubach, one of the best-known ministers throughout the entire world, asking him to preside over their wedding. Dr. Laubach was known throughout the planet as "the apostle to the illiterates." He was the author of some of the deepest, most devout books written in modern times, and he had been attributed with helping at least 250 million people learn to read and write because of the Laubach method.

Dr. Laubach had said yes.

Dr. Laubach's son, Bob, had been a friend of the groom's for a good number of years, and he had also agreed that he and his wife, Fran, would drive from Syracuse, New York, to be best man and matron of honor at the ceremony.

Then came the fairy-tale part. Just before going on the air, the couple was told that NBC had decided to end the coverage of the McCarthy hearings and throw open all their affiliated television stations. That meant that people all over America who turned on their televisions on May 13 would find the McCarthy hearings on ABC and CBS, but they would be able to watch *Bride and Groom* on NBC.

NBC told the couple, "Now that we have opened all the NBC television affiliate channels, we are certain there will be at least ten million people watching you being married this morning."

Dr. Laubach was fantastic. It was a performance worthy of any potentate joining a couple in holy matrimony. The bride and groom gave testimony of their faith in Jesus Christ and their calling to serve the Lord. The young couple also received a large number of gifts that were shown on television. They included a week-long honeymoon at the Barbizon Plaza Hotel (now known as Trump Towers), a car to be used by the young couple for the entire week, an electric range, an automatic dishwasher, a set of sterling silver, and a 16-mm motion picture of their wedding.

I have never learned how to use a computer, but I am told that today if you know how to use Google, you can inquire about a television program called *Bride and Groom*. If you are even more adept in the use of your computer, you can ask who was married that enchanted morning of May 13, 1954.

You may be surprised to discover that the beautiful young lady is named Helen, and on that day Gene and Helen Edwards were married in the presence of more than ten million people, including virtually the entire television viewing audience in all the state of Texas.

If you do the math, you will know just how long the couple who lived out this fairy-tale wedding have been married and how long they have been desperately in love. (It has been a fairy-tale marriage, too, and has gotten even better with age.)

# CHAPTER 7

## JONAH REVISITED

His name was James Bartley. He was a sailor who would become an evangelist. The scene of this truly remarkable story was off the coast of the Falkland Islands around 1880.

James was just another homeless, faceless person doing a thankless job on a whaling expedition and would have long-since been forgotten except for one life-changing event.

Someone in the crow's nest spotted a whale. Two boats were lowered. The two whale boats made fast toward the whale. A few moments later one of the men stepped out into something the whalers called the pulpit. It is a long stretch of steps leading out to the bow of the ship with a place to stand. A harpoon was thrown, and every man knew that the whaler had done his job well: the whale was now their captive. Nonetheless, the whale would not go down without a fight.

The whale slashed, turned, sounded, rose again, and began whipping one of the boats. Several men were knocked into the water. It was a long, furious fight. The whale was finally brought on board the great whaling ship. Two of the sailors recovered, surfaced, and swam to the ship. While the whale was systematically stripped, the rest of the crew searched the waters throughout the area in hopes of finding the missing sailor . . . or at least his floating body. The man who was missing was James Bartley.

The sailors worked through the night, first stripping the outer skin of the whale for one particular product that was in demand, then cutting into the deeper parts of the whale. One full day had passed. Someone thought they heard a sound coming from the whale. Thinking that was impossible, the report was ignored. Finally, after almost two full days, someone heard what truly did sound like a struggling breath. Disbelief continued, but nonetheless the men began furiously cutting away at the belly of the whale.

Eventually the outline of a human being could be seen.

A human body was finally recovered and pulled free from the whale's belly. What the men saw was a ghastly sight. The whale's stomach acids had begun to devour the flesh of James Bartley. Throughout the night there was a death watch set for James because everyone knew he could not survive.

Water was forced into his stomach. He was washed down again and again. His skin had been bleached by the gastric juices—the pigmentation was gone and parts of him looked like he had been born an albino.

How could he possibly have lived, separated from air, deep into the belly of the whale with its stomach juices eating away at his flesh? Still, after days of care, James recovered. He was sped home. This was the 1800s, when news moved very slowly. Nonetheless, tales began to spread of another Jonah. This happened in an era called "the enlightenment," when people were beginning to entertain the idea that there were errors in the Old Testament.

When James's strength returned and he found out that some people were saying the biblical story of Jonah being swallowed by a whale and surviving could not possibly be true, James was indignant. He began to visit churches, telling his completely unbelievable story. It was not long before James was traveling all over England giving his testimony, and, as the story goes, he called men and women to repentance and invited them to give up their doubts and turn to God.

Some of those Old Testament stories could not possibly be true?

# CHAPTER 8

# THE MAN THEY COULD
# NOT HANG

This story begins in the early part of the twentieth century. There was a well-to-do woman who lived alone in England, whose residence was called the Glen. One night she was hideously murdered.

The police immediately went to work to find out who had murdered this much-loved and respected woman. She had servants, but on this particular night, it was determined that there was only one other person in the house. That gentleman automatically became the prime suspect. The man's name was John Lee. Immediately, John began to tell everyone, "I am not guilty; I did not do this!"

But justice does not always see clearly.

Previously John had been brought up on a charge somewhere else for petty theft. John looked guilty in the eyes of everyone who wanted justice. He was tried, and again and again John pleaded his innocence. Then he was sentenced to be hanged. Upon hearing the sentence, right there in the courtyard he cried out, "You can't hang me; I'm innocent! I will never hang!"

Months passed and the day of his execution drew closer and closer. John continued crying his innocence and with absolute fury he would say, "God will not allow me to be hanged because I'm innocent. You can't hang me; it can't be done. I am innocent, and God will not allow it."

Extra precautions were taken to make sure the scaffold was in perfect condition. When the time of execution arrived, John was led up the steps, final words were spoken, and even with the cloth over his face, John screamed out, "I am innocent and you cannot hang me!"

The lever was pulled, and just as John had predicted,

the trap door did not work. He cried out again, "You can't hang me! God will not allow it." The police and everyone else in charge rechecked the entire scaffolding. The lever worked perfectly; there was no flaw in the mechanism.

John was brought up the stairs again, once more under protest. The lever was pulled, but John was left standing with the rope around his neck. Once more he was removed from the scaffold.

This time, one of the policemen stood on the trap door to test it, while others placed cushions to soften his fall. The lever was pulled and the policeman fell through the trap door and onto the cushions beneath. Then they weighed John, retrieved a sack that weighed exactly the same as John, put the sack exactly where John would be standing, pulled the lever, and the sack fell through the trap door.

Now for the third time, John was led up the stairs to the place where the trap door was, and once more he cried out, "You cannot hang me! I am innocent." Once more the lever was pulled, and once more the trap door did not open.

John fainted from the ordeal.

In our day, someone would say, "This has turned into cruel and unusual punishment."

The minister of England's homeland intervened and commuted John's sentence to life in prison. John spent twenty-two years in jail for a crime he did not commit.

Then, new facts began to emerge. The new science of forensics was being developed. It turned out that there possibly had been another man in the house at the time of the murder. Further, there were several things about the case that supported John's story of what happened that night.

Eventually John was cleared and released. There was other evidence which could not be used in court; nonetheless, it thundered John's innocence.

After John was released, he went straight to his church and told his story. He told it with great fervor. People in other places began asking him to tell his story. Soon all England would hear John Lee's story. John came to be known as "the man they could not hang."

Over and again, John told other Christians about his amazing experience and then dared atheists and agnostics to find any other explanation than that it was the hand of God that had saved him.

"I knew I was innocent, and God would not let me die."

No one ever argued with him about that.

# CHAPTER 9

# A CAN OF ORANGES

His name is Hubert Mitchell. He was without question one of the most awesome and formidable men I will ever know. The day I met him, the two things that stood out the most were his booming voice and the fact that he had no inhibitions.

Hubert was a missionary whose calling was to places where no one had ever heard of the gospel, and further, to go into the depths of the worst jungles on the earth and preach to tribes that did not even know there was a God. He went to the wild Kubu tribe in Sumatra when it was almost impossible to get to that isolated and forsaken island.

Some of the stories Hubert told defied belief, but my purpose for meeting him had nothing to do with his work as a missionary. His reputation, as far as I knew, lay in the fact that he was known to be one of the most effective personal soul winners.

I met Hubert when he was old. In Hubert's declining years, he had moved out of the jungles of Sumatra to the jungle of downtown Chicago. Hubert met with groups of businessmen once a week in Chicago's Loop and set up an incredible witness to those men. It was a gathering of some of the most influential men in Chicago. Hubert treated that area as if it were the center of a country village and he a country pastor.

I flew from Texas to Chicago to meet Hubert. I was a young man looking for anyone who could teach me an effective way to speak to others about Christ. Up until then I did not know how to lead others to Christ—nor did anyone else I knew.

Hubert met me at O'Hare Airport. He had agreed to take me with him as he went door-to-door. (I did not know what "door-to-door" meant to this man!)

Hubert parked his car downtown when we left the airport and asked, "Do you want to start right now?"

I agreed.

He looked at the dozen skyscrapers which surrounded us on every side. After a moment he announced, "I have never been in this one."

Hubert had picked one of the tallest buildings I had ever seen. To my chagrin, when we entered the elevator, Hubert pressed the button to the highest floor. The elevator door opened to the receptionist of the president and owner of said skyscraper.

"Good evening. I am a Christian minister, and I meet each week with men who work in the Loop. I would like to have a word of prayer with the president."

The receptionist and I were tied as to which of us was more dumbfounded. Still startled, she pressed a button on the phone and said, "Sir, there is a man here who wants to pray with you."

The reply from the intercom was instant! "Send him in."

Bold as brass, Hubert started around the desk of the receptionist, who caught up with Hubert and escorted him to the office of the president.

I, in turn, was apoplectic.

As I staggered to a chair, my entire world as a personal evangelist changed forever. About half an hour later, Hubert returned. He thanked the receptionist and turned to me, saying, "He will be with us in our next meeting."

I was too stupefied to say anything.

Everything I had been taught and read about witnessing died that night. Hubert did not have any particular "way." He lived with the expectation that the people he spoke to wanted to receive Christ as their Savior. Hubert had only one subject—to talk about Christ.

In R. A. Torrey's famous book *How to Bring Men to Christ*, Torrey told readers to quote Scripture because it is the power of God unto salvation. If there was resistance, quote Scripture; it was, again, the power of God unto salvation. Actually, this way usually led to an argument. Torrey's underlying thought was, first, the supposition that people would be resistant to the gospel and, second, that the power of Scripture alone would cause them to be converted.

Then, and even today, I challenged this supposition, but the fact was that my fellow pastors at the time were not doing any better than I had been doing at winning people to Christ.

After witnessing to the gentleman who owned the skyscraper, Hubert drove us to a neighborhood where he would go door-to-door with the expectation that some of the people would invite us into their living rooms.

"My name is Hubert Mitchell and I am a Christian. I would like to come in and have prayer with you and your family."

Sure enough, they opened the door. We went in and I watched Hubert Mitchell lead a man to Christ.

Hubert always talked about Jesus. He did not quote Scripture; he just kept on the subject of Jesus. You could not get him off the subject of Jesus Christ. From Hubert, I learned one of the most valuable things I have ever learned throughout my entire life. It is not logic nor reasoning; it is not verses of Scripture to put down arguments, for no argument ever came up. The most powerful thing in this universe in leading other people to the Lord is the Lord Himself. You could tell that Hubert was a man full of Christ; no one needed to tell you. Out of his Christ-centered life and his Christ-centered witness, Hubert had loosed the secret of soul winning: that is, to present Christ.

I was twenty-four. Something had changed in my life forever: *It is Christ, it is Christ, in all things it is Christ.* Never an *it*, but a *who.*

Today I often quote, "In every man there is a God-shaped vacuum that nothing can fill except Jesus Christ."

I left Chicago a different man. Back in Texas, I found witnessing to others a delight and a joy. Fellow pastors asked me to come to their churches to help them win others to Christ. Eventually I wrote *Here's How to Win Souls.* Soon I was holding county-wide, weeklong meetings for training others in personal evangelism. Then came city-wide campaigns in door-to-door evangelism.

And the genesis of all this: "Good afternoon. My name is Hubert Mitchell. I would like a prayer with the president of your company."

<hr>

One evening Hubert fell to telling me stories of his time as a missionary in the jungles of Sumatra. One of the stories he told was hilarious.

"I was walking along a trail in the jungle when I realized someone was strolling along beside me. I looked down. It was a tiger! He walked along with me for about a hundred feet and then turned back into the jungle. If he had paused to eat lunch, I would not be here today."

The next story is one of coincidence . . . or is it?

Hubert went into the deepest, most unreachable part of Sumatra. He took nothing but an interpreter and a sack slung over his shoulder containing food for the trek. He walked into a village and asked to meet with the chief. The chief listened intently. Hubert came to the point where he said, "And Jesus was nailed to a cross and died for your sins and mine, that we might be forgiven of our sins."

The chief of the tribe looked puzzled. It was the word *nailed* that he did not understand. So, the two men were stuck. Without understanding the word *nailed*, the chief could not understand the crucifixion and death of Jesus Christ. The part about dying on a tree, the chief could understand, but the nail he could not understand.

That evening Hubert sat down under a tree. He had a pack with him that was full of food. He looked in the pack to see if there was something else to finish the meal. Sure enough, there was a can of oranges. Hubert took out his can opener and opened his can of oranges. He began picking one of the peeled oranges out and eating it. He thought he heard a metallic sound. He reached in again to pull out another orange, and once again he heard a metallic sound. Curious, he began poking his finger around in the can of oranges. Lo and behold, Hubert Mitchell found a nail in his can of oranges!

He ate the rest of the oranges and put the empty can back into his pack. He sat there and stared at a nail that had no business being in Sumatra and certainly not in a can of oranges which had been manufactured in Japan.

The next day Hubert came to the chief. The chief stared at the nail, felt the point on one end, examined the blunt place where men might strike that nail and drive it through a wrist. Now the chief understood how Jesus Christ was nailed to a tree. The chief stood up and asked to receive Christ as Lord.

A few weeks later, having tested the waters of salvation, the chief shared the gospel with his tribe, which until this time had no god, and told them to each and all receive Christ as their Savior because now Jesus Christ was the God of this tribe. It was not unusual for the chief of a tribe, having received the Lord, to tell his entire tribe in turn to receive Christ as their Savior. The tribe would follow their chief in fully believing.

Today there is a jungle tribe in Sumatra which became Christian because of the most extraordinary circumstance.

There are Christian men, heads of large corporations, in the jungle of Chicago, who found Christ because a barrel-chested man with a commanding baritone voice led them to Him.

Hubert also taught a twenty-four-year-old young man how to lead others to Christ. Hubert, may your influence live on for years to come.

# CHAPTER 10

# GREAT DISCOVERERS

Christopher Columbus was sailing toward the Americas but did not know it. He thought he was going to end up in India. One day at sea his crew came and laid out their demands: he must turn back that same day. The men felt strongly that they were about to sail off the edge of a flat earth. Christopher Columbus made a deal: one more day and he would turn back.

Columbus did not know this, but he was not very far from an island, a place today we call San Salvador. San Salvador is about ten thousand miles away from

India. Columbus took a gold coin and nailed it to the mast, telling the crew that whoever saw land first would receive this coin. (It was not to be.) So it was that far into the night the men stared into the darkness hoping to see something. Columbus said he thought he had seen a flickering light. He had not. It was impossible for any artificial light to be that far away. Up in the crow's nest, a sailor named Rodrigo de Triana saw land and called out "Tierra! Tierra!" ("Land! Land!")

Everyone was excited and the ship was turned in the direction of Rodrigo's sighting. Only a few minutes later several other men called out that they had seen land. Within no more than thirty minutes everyone was aware that they could see the outline of a small mountain range.

You will have to search very hard to find Rodrigo in history books, and that is because Columbus claimed the coin. The truth of the matter is simple: Rodrigo was the first man to sight the Americas on that voyage.

A man named Enrique of Malacca was living in the Philippines. He was captured by slave traders and shipped to India. There he was placed on the slave market. About this same time, but half a world away, a young lieutenant in the Spanish Navy sailed out of Gibraltar on a ship that was determined to reach India and possibly even meet sailors from the mysterious land of China.

Sailing south for what seemed forever, the ship came to the Cape of Good Hope and sailed around the southernmost part of the West Coast of Africa. The captain of the ship was determined to reach India. Now sailing north around the east side of Africa, the ship at last docked at a harbor in India. The young sailor stepped off the ship. He had come almost halfway around the world. That would be as far as he would ever go, sailing from West to East.

There were several discoveries made there by the ship and its captain. The lieutenant saw, for the first time ever, the sampans of China. He and his fellow sailors were seeing a place where the spices and herbs of this mysterious East were being bought. There was something else discovered there—a Christian church. No one knew that. After much translating and comparing notes, the men realized that there were truly Christians in India. They also were told that it was no less than Thomas the Apostle who had traveled this far and planted the gospel and the church. The Christians were neither Roman Catholics nor Eastern Orthodox.

One of the things the young lieutenant, whose name was Ferdinand Magellan, did while he was there was purchase a slave. The slave had originally come from the Philippines, been captured, shackled, and brought west to the slave markets of India. The slave Enrique would now be Magellan's constant companion.

What the crew did not know was that the people there were planning to kill everyone on that ship, sink it, and make sure that word never got back to Europe that the ship had reached India. The knowledge of the Indian Ocean would never be known in Europe.

On the very next morning, the killing began. The Spanish captain of the ship was killed, along with most of the crew. Magellan, a lieutenant, quickly boarded ship and, with the few men who were still alive, hoisted sails and made their way out of the seaport.

It was a long, long journey back down the side of Africa to return to the Cape of Good Hope to sail again to the north and come at last to the Strait of Gibraltar.

Magellan's report was simple. "The world is far

bigger than we ever dreamed it was. We have not yet reached China."

He believed the best route was not to go east from Spain and Portugal but to sail west, find the southern end of this new American continent, then sail *west* across the Pacific Ocean, finally arriving in China. For years Magellan promoted this. Finally, he was given permission by King Charles I of Spain and was given the money to sail. Again, his slave Enrique was by his side.

What would happen next must be one of history's most arduous sailing expeditions. By the time Magellan, now the captain of this exploratory mission, and his five ships reached the east coast of South America and had turned south to find what are now called the Strait of Magellan, he had put down a mutiny by three of his captains. His men were discouraged, out of food, and suffering from dysentery. Magellan did not realize that most of the hellish trip still lay ahead of them.

Over and over his three remaining ships sought to find a passageway through the islands at the southern-most tip of South America. Over and again they had to turn back and sail farther south, always to be met only with a dead end to the path they had chosen. Finally, on November 28, 1520, the ships entered the South Pacific.

For four months Magellan sailed northwest across the Pacific. The only nourishment they had came from boiling the leather straps found on the sails and chewing on them. On a few occasions, a tiny island would be found, some food would be gathered and placed in the hull of the ship, and they would valiantly move on.

On March 16, 1521, Magellan's ships landed in Cebu on the Philippines. Magellan's slave was home. No one seemed to understand this at the moment, but Magellan's slave was the first person to ever circumvent the world (because Magellan's own circumvention would not be complete until he made it all the way to India).

However, this slave betrayed Magellan. A plot was hatched when Magellan left his ship to walk ashore one particular morning. The natives, led by the slave, started a furious fight and Magellan was clubbed to death. Magellan never went around the world, but Magellan's slave, Enrique of Malacca, did. And the man who first set eyes on the east coast of the Americas (a Bahamian island) from a crow's nest was Rodrigo de Triana.

Matthew Alexander Henson was born on August 8, 1866. He was the son of two American freeborn black sharecroppers. At the age of eleven he left home, found work as a cabin boy, was educated by the captain who took him under his wing, and as a young man saw much of the world, traveling to Asia, Africa, and Europe.

In 1884, he met Robert Edwin Peary, an explorer. Impressed by Henson's seafaring credentials, Peary hired him and he joined Peary for an expedition to Greenland. Over the next several years, Peary and Henson would make multiple attempts to reach the North Pole. The final attempt began in 1908. The expedition was large, leaving Greenland on August 18 with "22 Inuit men, 17 Inuit women, 10 children, 246 dogs, 70 tons of whale meat, the meat and blubber of 50 walruses, hunting equipment, and tons of coal." Eight months later, on April 6, 1909, Peary established "Camp Jesup" within five miles of the North Pole. He then selected Henson and four Inuit men as part of the team of six who would make the final run to the Pole. Before the goal was reached, Peary could no longer continue on foot and rode in a dog sled. Various accounts say he was ill, exhausted, or had frozen toes. He sent Henson on ahead as a scout.

In a later newspaper interview, Henson would say: "I was in the lead that had overshot the mark a couple of miles. We went back then, and I could see that my footprints were the first at the spot."

Henson then proceeded to plant the American flag.

---

So it is that we have three: Rodrigo, the first to see the "New World"; Enrique, the first man to go around the world; and Matthew, the first person to actually stand on top of the North Pole. However, they are only footnotes in the history books. The credit went to Columbus, Magellan, and Peary.

In this footnote to history, however, there is something else that must be added: All three of these men were black. Rodrigo was born in Africa; Enrique was of a black colony in Cebu, Philippines; Matthew Henson was African American.

# CHAPTER 11

# HIS OPEN EYES
# OPENED MINE

I have told you the story of the fairy-tale wedding of Gene and Helen Edwards. There was something else that took place during that same trip to New York City. When we arrived we had an invitation from Dr. Frank Laubach to have dinner with him the night before the television wedding. We were stunned. Here was one of the best-known and most-revered men in the world. He had been a missionary and developed a worldwide literacy program. In 1984 he became the only American missionary to be honored on a US postage stamp, and we were going to have dinner with him.

After dinner, Dr. Laubach invited Helen and me up to his apartment. The thing I remember the most when we walked into his home was seeing the various awards he had received. One was a plaque engraved by the sponsors with the simple words: "Frank Laubach, Man of the Year."

There was no way that I could possibly know the changes that would pass through my life that evening. I was a zealous young man who had but one ambition in life. It was a very small ambition: to evangelize the entire planet during my lifetime.

"Something would happen in Dr. Laubach's home that evening which which would begin to change the direction of my life. As we started to leave, I asked Dr. Laubach to lay hands on Helen and me and pray for us. He was seated in a chair, and Helen and I knelt before him, allowing him to lay his hands on us.

What happened after that is a little difficult to explain.

I heard words. I had never heard anything like what I was hearing.

Unknowingly, I had become used to the perfunctory praying of Christians of my era. That was not what I was hearing. I was hearing someone talk to a very near-and-dear close friend. There was no pretense in the prayer; in fact, it was in no sense a prayer. This was a person who knew someone else intimately.

I opened my eyes. When I say "I opened my eyes," you can take that on two levels.

I saw Frank Laubach praying with his eyes open, and he was looking up in a way that one could easily be convinced he was looking into the face of God.

I had been kneeling there with both of my hands clutched together, my whole body was tight, I was praying with great fervency. On the other hand, the man I saw, and the words I heard, were unlike anything I had ever known in any dimension anywhere at any time. There, kneeling before Dr. Laubach with his hands on Helen and me, I received my very first glimpse of a totally different way of relating to the Lord.

That was the beginning of a change in my spiritual life. It was the beginning of my gradually coming to know a little about other realms, of the unseen realm and things of a spiritual nature.

But the story doesn't end there.

Several years later, when I was in my late thirties, I picked up the phone and called Bob Laubach, Dr. Frank Laubach's son. Dr. Laubach had already gone to be with the Lord. I asked Bob if I could take one of Dr. Laubach's books, a little book out of print and out of copyright, and add it to another book. Both of the books were too small to sell particularly well in bookstores. They were more like pamphlets.

The first was a four-hundred-year-old treatise titled "Practicing the Presence of God."

Dr. Laubach's book was also written about trying to follow the Lord's admonitions to practice the presence of Jesus Christ. The two pamphlets were made for each other.

Bob granted his permission, so I published the two books together under the title *Practicing His Presence*. I had no idea how the new book would be received. I had rewritten much of both books; I updated them and added clarification where needed. I had taken the writings of two of the most devout Christians in church history, Brother Lawrence and Frank Laubach, and turned them into a book that was a little more logically organized for the modern reader and less difficult to read and the information thus available to more people.

The process I went through of taking a book that is four hundred years old and modernizing it alongside Dr. Laubach's book had such an impact that it changed the course of my life. I came to know that a deep, intimate, personal relationship with Jesus Christ is possible and is more important than anything else.

And it all began in a New York apartment in 1954 when my spiritual eyes were opened while Dr. Frank Laubach was praying with his physical eyes wide open. Something was born in me the night he prayed for us.

Today I am the same age as Frank Laubach was on the day he joined Helen and me in marriage.

Something of what Brother Lawrence wrote nearly four hundred years ago and what Dr. Laubach wrote almost a hundred years ago was planted in me and has made a home in my inmost being.

I speak across the centuries: "Thank you, dear precious brothers, for planting something in my heart when I was young."

# CHAPTER 12

# DON'T BE IN SUCH AN "ALL-FIRED RUSH"

One of the most amazing people I have ever met in my life was a gentleman named Gerri Von Frellick. Gerri was an entrepreneur personified. He built large shopping centers in different parts of America. What I learned from Gerri was that it doesn't matter how big the problem is, there has to be a solution.

Gerri told me this story while we were having dinner at his home. His wife was present, and she was helping him tell the story.

Gerri's home was in Denver, Colorado. While sitting at his desk in his office, he got a call. There was some property that he wished to purchase in Colorado Springs and the property had come up for sale. Unless Gerri got there within the next two hours, someone else would purchase the property at a slightly cheaper price. Gerri grabbed his car keys and headed for the Denver airport.

You must understand that these were far more informal days back in the 1950s. Gerri arrived at the airport as the plane to Colorado Springs was about to depart. There were no security checks in those days. In fact, the first security checks that America would ever know would be coming in just a few days.

Gerri ran up the gangplank at the same time they were closing the door to the airplane. This was not a jet or even a large prop plane, this was a small but often-hailed DC3.

There was a story told about the DC3 in World War II: "If someone shoots that plane in half, you can be sure that the DC3 could land with half of it, and if you wait about ten or fifteen minutes, the other half will land too."

The DC3 was a plane that was hard to crash. One of the reasons was that the two engines were totally separated from each other and shared no common dependency. Further, if one engine went out, the plane would fly just as well with one engine.

Has anyone ever said to you: "It is impossible for that to happen," "That can't happen," or "That's never happened before"?

Gerri sat down in the plane and announced that he had no ticket but he was not going to get off the plane. Sure enough, the crew made arrangements for Gerri to buy a ticket while sitting right there in the airplane. A few minutes later they were airborne.

Gerri was watching his wristwatch. It was a short flight from Denver to Colorado Springs. And then something happened that could not happen, had never happened before, and is impossible to happen: One of the DC3 engines went out. Then, five minutes later, the other engine went out. In any other airplane on earth that would have spelled disaster, but the DC3 had such a long wing span that when the engines were gone it became a glider.

A few moments later the pilot safely landed the DC3

in a cornfield. In fact, the plane was right beside a highway connecting Denver to Colorado Springs. Gerri got out of the plane, hitchhiked a ride, and got to the realtor's office just in time to write a check and purchase the property.

Shortly after that near-disaster, his wife said, "Gerri, let this be a lesson to you: don't be in such an all-fired rush."

Gerri did not know that a few short days later that sentence would save his life. Gerri's wife drove him to the airport and made sure he had purchased his ticket before she went back to the car and drove away, certain that Gerri would be on a DC6 airplane from Denver to Los Angeles. He was waiting for the flight to be announced so he could board the plane.

A flight attendant called everyone together and stated, "We are overbooked. Is there anyone who would be so kind as to give your seat to someone else? There will be another flight in two hours on another airline, and we will make arrangements for you to be on that airplane."

Gerri heard an echo in his mind: "Gerri, let that teach you a lesson, don't be in such an all-fired rush!"

Totally out of character, Gerri agreed to wait two hours for the next flight. In those days, no one made any promises of a second ticket, a free trip, or extra flight miles; it was just a courtesy.

What no one knew was that a madman had placed a bomb in a piece of luggage in the belly of the first plane.

Back in those days, there was a machine you could walk up to and purchase insurance. For example, $20 might get you $250,000 worth of insurance. Of course, no one dreamed that anyone could be so cruel as to blow up a plane in order to collect insurance on the death of a family member who was booked on a flight. But, shortly after the plane took off, it blew up in the sky not far from Denver.

Surprisingly, Gerri did not hear about this before he caught the next plane to Los Angeles. In the meantime, his wife had been called and told that the plane Gerri was on had crashed and there were no survivors. Remember, this was before cell phones and TVs seemingly everywhere, so Gerri knew nothing about all this.

Meanwhile, Gerri safely arrived in Los Angeles, went to his hotel, and a few minutes later started to pull back the covers and instead decided to call his wife and tell her goodnight. The phone rang and Gerri said, "Hi, sweetheart."

His wife began to scream, "You're dead! You're dead!"

Gerri had no idea what was happening.

After a few moments Mrs. Von Frellick calmed down and explained that the airplane he had booked a seat on had blown up in the sky. If Gerri had not offered to wait two hours for another plane, he would have been dead and Mrs. Von Frellick would have been a widow.

When Gerri and his wife told me this story, it did not fall on deaf ears. I have been one of those people who have always been in an "all-fired rush."

Gerri had calmed down a great deal. So did I.

There was always the opportunity to wait, to yield, to give up, and give Providence an opportunity to work its way.

So, I share a simple thought: *Don't be in such an all-fired rush!*

# CHAPTER 13

# WILL DAUGHTER BE
# LIKE MOTHER?

A young doctor had just started his medical practice. One of his first patients was a young man about his age named Jim. Over the years, the two of them, both professionals, became very close friends. Jim married a girl named Deborah. The doctor became the family physician. Jim and Deborah then conceived a child, a baby girl whom they named Alicia. The doctor brought that child into the world. Alicia grew up and she also had a girl, Katlyn, for her first child. The doctor was now the family physician for three generations of girls.

One day the youngest in the family, Katlyn, a lovely eighteen-year-old girl, came to the doctor's office. She had something she wanted to talk with him about, but not until he would promise to tell no one. She told her story of having fallen in love. Then came the difficult part: "I'm pregnant, I'm not married, and I don't know what to do."

The doctor and the young lady talked for a long, long time.

Because of professional ethics, the doctor could not tell Katlyn what he so badly wanted to tell her. She left the office. He walked over to his filing cabinets and found the records of another young girl who had come to see him about nineteen years earlier. He opened her file and saw on the first page the notation he had made then: "Unmarried, pregnant twenty-year-old. I know her father and her mother. She is undecided about telling them she is pregnant and that the young father does not want to marry. Alicia is considering the possibility of an abortion. I pray to God she will not do that."

On the second page, two weeks later, he had written, "Prayers answered! Alicia has decided to keep the baby."

As he prepared to file the records for his most recent patient, once more the doctor penned a note, "I pray that Katlyn will make the same decision her mother made years ago and give birth to life and not destroy it."

I wish I could tell Katlyn that her mother almost made a decision to destroy her before she was born.

# CHAPTER 14

# TWO AMAZING CONVERSIONS

Two of the most amazing stories of conversions to Christ I have ever heard are recounted here. The first one I knew very little about, but when I finally met the man, I paused long enough to ask, "Is the story of your conversion true?"

He replied in the affirmative and then shared his brief testimony. He had been caught up in a tornado. The tornado carried him about five hundred feet up in the air and dropped him. He said that when the tornado picked him up, he had not been a Christian, but when the tornado deposited him in a tree, he was a Christian!

John Wesley once said: "A man can be riding a horse, fall off of the horse, and by the time he hits the ground he has received Jesus Christ as his Savior."

Have you ever felt that the Lord intervened in the course of the affairs of the world to work His will in one small event? This second story is just such a story.

William, a young college student, was approached by the Navigators, a Christian group headquartered in Colorado Springs, Colorado, who began witnessing to William about Jesus Christ. William was adamant that he was not interested and he did not want to hear any more about Jesus. Several tries by the Navigators ended up just as futile. Then one of these young men dared to do a very foolish thing. In fact, I would never recommend it.

The young Navigator said to William, "What would it take for you to receive Christ as your Savior?"

What an encompassing question that was, and William answered in kind. William made reference to a baseball club. It was a new club that had taken the place of the Los Angeles Dodgers when they moved from

Brooklyn to the West Coast. This new baseball team was called the New York Mets. The first seven years they never had a winning season and were the laughing stock of the entire baseball world. Yet, they had as loyal a following as any baseball team in America. People came to watch the Mets fail, cheer them on, and relish in telling the stories of how bad the team was.

Then William let loose with his response. "I will take your Lord Jesus Christ as my Lord and Savior, I will get down on my knees and ask Him to come into my life to save me and wash me from my sins if next year the Mets win the pennant and then go on to win the World Series."

This was an absolute impossibility in the minds of everyone in the baseball world.

In the spring of 1969 the new season began. Throughout the year the Mets seemed to be losing almost every game they played but often pulled out a win in the last few innings. Then, to everyone's astonishment, they managed to win their division title and the National League pennant and finally made it to the World Series.

Of course, no one believed they could win the World

Series! After all, they would be up against the Baltimore Orioles, who that year won an astonishing 109 regular season games and had stars at almost every position. They were considered to be one of the finest teams there had ever been and had been a club for fifty years.

The World Series started. The Mets lost the first game. But they won the next three and in the final game won by the score of 5 to 3, scoring 5 runs in the last three innings. The Mets had won the World Series and would earn the nickname "Miracle Mets," replacing their former nickname "Lovable Losers."

So it was that the two Navigators subsequently approached William and said, "William, you gave your word."

William kept that word. He actually got down on his knees and asked Jesus Christ to come into his life.

As William told me this story, I felt sure that the entire 1969 baseball season had been in the hands of God just for one reason, and that reason was to see William find Jesus Christ as his Savior.

William, now called Bill, went on to be a home missionary working among Native Americans in one of the most isolated places in America. In fact, he had to drive two hundred miles to get to the closest grocery store.

Did the Mets really win the 1969 World Series just so . . . ?

Bill died as I was writing this chapter, and I cannot help but believe that he went to be with the Lord with angels waiting to hear him tell this story in person.

# CHAPTER 15

# THE DIRT FARMER

It was the early 1800s. A Virginian had been work-ing out on his farm all day long. He had named his home Monticello. Late in the afternoon he received a delegation of statesmen from the capital of Virginia. There were some serious conflicts and problems in the state. The delegation had turned to this man, so respected not only in Virginia but throughout America. The problem presented to the farmer was enough to concern him so much that he decided he would ride through the evening to the capital to help resolve the crisis. Along the way he would see if he could find a place to eat and sleep. If not, he would ride his horse through the night and into the next day.

As evening first began its advance, the dirt farmer, who had not made any effort to change his clothing, came to a tavern. He went in and sat down at a table to order food. As dirty as he was, no one recognized him. Perhaps his hat covered his flaming red hair.

The innkeeper took one look at him and said, "I don't serve dirt farmers here, and you will get no food and you will get no lodging."

The tall man rose and, without saying a word, left to continue his journey to the capital of Virginia. He found both food and shelter farther down the road.

Just a few days later, the innkeeper, who had shown no kindness nor consideration toward the wayfarer, discovered who the man was. He immediately dispatched a letter which read, "I am so sorry I did not know who you were. I ask you to return and allow us to extend to you the hospitality of our inn and show you every consideration which you so amply deserve."

A few days later the innkeeper received a letter from one of America's best-known citizens. The letter read,

"Sir, if you do not know how to extend kindness and hospitality to a dirt farmer, you will also not know how to give hospitality to the vice president of the United States."

Signed, Thomas Jefferson.

We have all been taught to be kind and thoughtful to others. In this story we could say, "This is not the way to do it." It is an example of how never to be rude or short, arrogant or quick-tempered with those who need hospitality, because we may be dealing with someone whose place in society we could not imagine.

Next is the remarkable story of a young man who extended kindness and hospitality to strangers who were so impressed with his thoughtfulness that they changed his life forever.

# CHAPTER 16

# THE POWER
# OF HOSPITALITY

It was late at night in the early 1900s at a small hotel in Philadelphia. The weather outside was wintry cold. An elderly couple came in, approached the desk, and asked if there was a room. The young man behind the desk, George Boldt, explained that there was a convention in town and there would be no rooms available anywhere in the city. The couple turned to leave, but George called out to them, "Sir, I cannot possibly turn you out on a night like this. I have a personal room of my own I keep in this hotel, but I will not be using it this night. Please, let me give you my room for tonight."

The couple agreed. He then provided some dinner for them, showing every courtesy a man could possibly give to perfect strangers. The next morning, he provided them with breakfast at no charge.

The couple showed a great deal of interest in George. The elderly gentleman asked for George's name and his address, so that he would be able to contact him in the future to show his appreciation. George gave the gentleman his name and information and thought nothing of it again . . . until he received a most mysterious letter.

The elderly couple he had helped had been very impressed with George. Enclosed was some money, a train ticket to New York City, and an address. If he would let them know when he could make the trip, they would send a limousine to pick him up.

George made the trip, and when the limousine pulled up, the couple stepped out and introduced themselves, although their names had little meaning for George. Getting back into the limousine, the three of them were driven to downtown New York, and there, under construction, was one of the largest hotels in America.

The gentleman said to George, "I am building a hotel, and I would like for you to manage it. Take the kind of hospitality that you showed to my wife and me and infuse that hospitality, those kindnesses and courtesies, into the entire staff."

The gentleman's name was of German extract; actually, he was named after a tiny village in the Black Forest in Germany. His given name was Waldorf, his last name was that of one of the wealthiest families in America: Astor.

Waldorf Astoria is one of the most luxurious hotel chains in the entire world. In fact, at the time of this story, it was the most lavish hotel in New York City.

George did indeed engender that courtesy, kindness, and thoughtfulness into the entire staff. To this day, Waldorf Astoria hotels and resorts are famous for the way they care for their guests.

This story has been told many times to make employees aware of courtesy to customers. It also reminds us of the oft-repeated statement, "Men have entertained angels unaware." The next story may literally be the reality of that statement.

# CHAPTER 17

# HOTEL ROOM 15

Her name was Marilyn Grosboll. She was a nurse with two master's degrees. Her two brothers and father were all doctors.

Marilyn had three names. At Santa Barbara City College, where she worked, she was respectfully called Ms. Grosboll. Her friends called her Marilyn, but those of us who knew her as one of the most devoted Christians we would ever know called her Grossy. Marilyn later came to meet with the Christians I met with, who all gathered in homes. She was much loved.

Marilyn had a very deep love for her Lord, so in the little college town of Isla Vista, California, she opened a restaurant called the Tree of Life. Any Christian in that town, and there were very few, would immediately recognize this as being a Christian café by its name. Marilyn's purpose was, of course, to witness to people who came into her restaurant.

I ventured in one evening and met Marilyn. I told her the entire story of the Tree of Life as I understood it in Scripture.

One evening, while I was dining at the Tree of Life with my wife, Marilyn sat down and told us this story.

Marilyn had been helping needy people in another city. One of the people she and her friends were working with was a young man whom we will call Les.

Les was a very needy young man. One day the friends who were caring for Les said that he had wandered off. Everyone was concerned. Les needed friends and he needed almost constant supervision. No one knew where he was, so Marilyn headed to the last street where he had been seen and drove down the street for a long distance. She stopped across the street from a gas station. She was about to go into the station when the door opened and a man stepped out.

"Sir, did you happen to see a young man walking down the street? His name is Les."

The man immediately responded and said, "Yes, if you go down one more block, you will find him in a hotel in Room 15."

Grossy drove her car to the hotel and walked in. There was no one at the desk. She looked down the hall, and the clerk had just opened the door to a hotel room to allow two people in. Grossy followed their steps, looking at each room number. Room 15 happened to be the very door that was being opened. The guest who was walking into his room announced that there was someone in there.

Grossy said, "Could it be a young man by the name of Les?"

"Say fella, is your name Les?"

Grossy heard his voice. "Yes."

A few moments later, Les was walking out to Grossy's car. He explained that he had walked into the hotel, he did not see the clerk anywhere, so he walked down the hall and saw a door slightly ajar, and it happened to be Room 15. So he went in.

Marilyn and Les drove back to the gas station. She started to go inside, and as she was about to open the door, a different man came out. Marilyn asked the name of the man who had come out earlier, describing the entire story to the proprietor of the gas station. He assured her that no such person had been there. She described him again, and once more the proprietor of the gas station said, "There is no such person here and never has been, and there would be no reason for that person to be in this room."

Grossy turned to Les, "Did you meet anyone here?"

"No," he replied.

"Did you tell anyone at any time that you were in Room 15?"

Les assured Grossy that no, nothing like that had happened.

If anyone else had told me this story I might have had doubts about its veracity. But not from Grossy.

In a way that is the end of the story. Now each of us must draw our own conclusions.

# CHAPTER 18

# REMEMBER PETER

Two years after World War II, Baptists opened a seminary in Zurich, Switzerland. There were students there from nineteen European nations. I had the privilege to be the one American representative at that school.

During the first semester, a student from Germany fell in love with a beautiful Christian girl who lived in Switzerland. He began dating her immediately and they were soon engaged. We all knew that they would be married, as engagement was tantamount to marriage.

In those days in Switzerland, engagement and marriage were inseparable. Therefore, when we heard that she was pregnant, we were not surprised. We knew their marriage would come immediately. What shocked us was her father's reaction. Her father refused to allow the couple to be married. His reason: the law in Zurich then was that if a child is born out of wedlock, the State pays for all expenses.

The faculty was shocked, the students were in shock, and everyone was on the side of the young ministerial student and his betrothed. But her father remained adamant. The baby was born, and the State paid the expenses. However, my friend's situation became worse when the girl's father then refused to allow the couple to marry even after the birth of the child.

What hurt so much was that Hans, the student from Germany, was one of the finest young men in the seminary. His fiancée, one of the most devout Christians among the small number of evangelical Christians in Zurich, was also held in great esteem. A year passed. I returned home to the United States. I often wondered whatever happened to Hans. I assumed that his life had been more or less ruined. One day I received a phone call from him; he was in the United States. I immediately invited him to speak at the church where I was the minister.

Hans explained that the girl's father never gave her permission to marry him. He eventually married a girl from Germany. He and his wife both felt called by God as missionaries to "foreign fields."

The story Hans told me was one of those experiences when grace was added to grace.

Hans had an appointment to present himself before an independent mission board here in the United States. Before asking for an appointment, he wrote a letter telling the board his entire story. He was waiting to receive their response.

Would he be given an interview? Would he even be considered for the mission field?

While Hans was visiting me, he received a response from the board. He gave me the unopened envelope. It contained only two words. Right in the middle of the page was written:

"Remember Peter!"

To see a mission board write a letter so powerful was proof that Hans had faced his past and made short and straight work of things that had taken place when he was young. It was also evidence that grace and forgiveness were in the hearts of the mission board.

<hr />

I heard another story when I was young of a famous judge. Someone viciously attacked him. He did not respond.

Later the attacker repented and wrote a letter asking forgiveness. The esteemed judge, a Christian, responded in handwriting with three words: *Forgiven. Forgotten. Forever.*

Words to be written on the heart: *Forgiven. Forgotten. Forever. Remember Peter!*

# CHAPTER 19

# THE PREACHER AND THE LYNCH MOB

As a boy growing up in Bay City, Texas, I became aware of the local legend of a preacher who came within seconds of being lynched by a mob. We boys even knew the exact location where he was about to be hanged from a railroad bridge. We also knew the preacher's name, Mordecai Ham.

In the 1930s there were two prominent evangelists well known throughout much of the United States. One was Billy Sunday, and the other was Mordecai Ham.

Mordecai Ham had preached the gospel across Texas, and Texans seemed to prefer him over Billy Sunday. Texas was also the place Ham liked to preach the most, and his favorite story was this one, which happened in Bay City, Texas.

The pastor of the First Baptist Church invited Mordecai to come to their city to preach the gospel. Mordecai Ham was known for his fervor and his zeal, and he was also known for preaching on more than the message of salvation through Jesus Christ. That is, he also preached against something that was called in those days "demon rum." This was just before prohibition became a reality. Billy Sunday, Mordecai Ham, and the Women's Temperance League were more or less responsible for the amendment to the Constitution that prohibited alcohol's being sold across state lines.

In the first year of Ham's ministry, some thirty-six thousand people received Jesus Christ as their Savior, which was amazing because he was invited to hold individual and city-wide campaigns, mostly in the sparsely populated smaller cities of America. In Bay City, Mordecai Ham preached as much outdoors as he did inside: on the town square, on street corners, and any place near a liquor store. His words concerning liquor were harsh and damning.

A highly offended group of men hatched a plot which, should they be successful, would end in the hanging of Mordecai Ham.

Having seized Mordecai Ham, they were assured that he would put up a violent fight to keep from being hanged. Nothing could have been further from the truth. Mordecai used this moment to preach the gospel to the men who were about to take his life. This mob led him out of the city to a place that had already been planned for the execution.

Just south of the city was a railroad. There was a place on the rails that required the track to be suspended over a stream. From the track to the water below was approximately twelve feet. The mob planned to put one end of a rope around his neck and the other end around the rail. They would push him off the track and Mordecai would die at the end of a dangling rope.

While he was waiting to be executed, Mordecai Ham never ceased preaching the gospel of Jesus Christ to these men.

Word reached the sheriff, and he started out to the

site, but no one was certain whether or not Mordecai would still be alive when the law arrived.

Sure enough, the rope had been tied around Mordecai Ham's neck at one end, with the other tied around the rail itself. The men were just about to fling him off the track when the sheriff and some good citizens of the city reached him and stopped the lynching.

Such was the story I often heard as a little boy. The world would be a very different place today had Mordecai Ham died that day. Here's why.

Dating back to the founding of the colonies, there has been a tradition in the United States of preachers speaking to large gatherings of people. They became known as "mass evangelists." The first two—in the 1700s—were John Wesley, the founder of the Methodist movement, and George Whitfield, whose crowds were even larger than those of John Wesley.

Nearly a century later came Charles Finney, one of the most wild-eyed, daring preachers who ever lived on this continent. After Charles Finney came Dwight L. Moody, who was received by massive crowds both in England and in the United States. He was also the founder of one of the two first Bible schools in America.

After Moody, the most notable person to come forth as a mass evangelist was Billy Sunday, who made his home in a small town in Illinois. None too far behind Billy Sunday was the also-noted evangelist Mordecai Ham.

Hearing this story as a child, I had no reason to think that I would ever meet Mordecai Ham nor come to know his most famous convert whose name is known throughout the entire world. But in my very first year in seminary, I was a counselor at the Billy Graham Crusade in Fort Worth, Texas, in 1951. It was just after that evangelistic crusade that ancient, much-venerated Mordecai Ham was speaking at a church in Fort Worth.

A legend from my childhood had come once more to Texas. I would have not missed meeting him for anything. So it was, I heard him tell the story of the day he was almost hanged and also the story of his most famous convert.

At the very apex of his ministry, Mordecai Ham had been invited to speak in Charlotte, North Carolina. The crowds were large, the man was thunderous, and his words were delivered with power. A good-sized group of young people listened to him. One of them was a sixteen-year-old boy named Bill.

Bill stepped forward to receive Christ. He grew up

to become one of the most famous and most important figures of the twentieth century. You will, of course, recognize his name as Billy Graham.

Mordecai Ham, who was almost hanged in the town I grew up in, led Billy Graham to Christ.

Billy Graham has been seen face-to-face more than any other man in history. He has been heard on television, radio, and in crusades more than any other human being that has ever lived on this planet. Through mass evangelism, he has led more people to Jesus Christ than anyone else in Christian history.

The day of Billy Sunday and Mordecai Ham has passed. Their breed of men is perhaps gone forever, but may men that brave and that bold never be forgotten.

# CHAPTER 20

# MEMBA

Don McClure hailed from Pennsylvania. The country where his mission organization sent him was Sudan. There he met Memba, the great witch doctor of that area and the tribes around. Sudan at this time was a land mostly of jungles and tribal peoples where few had ever heard the gospel.

On one particular day, McClure became aware of a palpable silence. He looked out his window and saw a large number of tribesmen sitting before his house. All, he was aware, believed in and were terrified of Memba.

A few moments later, Memba appeared. He was a big man and he had painted his body to look furious. He seemed to possess supernatural powers.

"I am Memba!" he cried out to McClure. "Come out of your house, stand and face me. I will show you what Memba can do. Then, McClure, you must show me what you can do."

The tribesmen cried out in agreement. There would be a test: one would win; the other would lose. At that moment, the results of the challenge seemed to favor Memba, who had spent years perfecting his magic.

Soon, McClure stepped through the door to accept the challenge. "Alright Memba, show us all what your great powers are. I will answer with the power of God."

Instantly Memba lifted high a hideous looking creature of the jungles. You and I would see it as a huge, poisonous tarantula. It seemed obvious that one bite from this jungle creature meant instant death. Memba held up the monstrous spider for all to see. By its very appearance this huge arachnid announced its murderous ability. Memba allowed this eight-legged creature to crawl all over his back, his neck, his chest, his arms, and even his face. Memba then held out the goliath tarantula and pointed it toward McClure as though he was handing it to him.

It was the moment of truth. Memba, a doctor of witch's brews, would win or the gospel would prevail.

McClure responded, "I will take your challenge, Memba."

He then announced that he was going back into his room to talk with his God, the one true and living God. McClure went back into his room and closed the door. He suspected that Memba had rubbed some kind of oil on his body, which caused the creature to not bite him. He knew that he himself had absolutely no idea how to counter this display of magic.

McClure bowed his head and was about to pray, but before he began, he saw something on his desk. He picked it up. "Possibly, just possibly, *this* is what the Lord has given me."

Sure that God had given him his answer even before he had asked, McClure turned toward the door, holding a magnifying glass in his hand.

With the confidence that the Lord had given him, McClure opened the door and stepped out to offer his challenge to Memba. At that moment, the sun was blistering hot. Very cautiously McClure slipped this childhood plaything out of his shirt, looked up at the sun, and calculated exactly where and at what angle to hold the magnifying glass.

McClure extended his hand. Memba dropped that hideous thing with the venom of death into the missionary's palm. There, for just an instance, he felt this hairy creature on his skin and knew that it would surely bite him if he did not act quickly. McClure focused his magnifying glass on the spider. Soon there was smoke and then fire. Then there was a crackling sound, and the creature burst into flames. McClure turned his hand and let the flaming spider fall to the ground dead.

The tribesmen saw it all and cried out in fear and astonishment. Watching his creature bursting into flames, Memba turned away. The two men had clashed, and Memba had been defeated.

Memba did not show himself in that area again. The people listened to McClure speak as the highest, most powerful person in their world. The task of preaching the gospel to the tribes had now changed from being difficult to being heard with great eagerness.

Jesus once said that the Holy Spirit already knows

what you are going to ask before you ask it. That is exactly what happened that day. His answer came in the form of a small magnifying glass.

God answered McClure even before he prayed.

# CHAPTER 21

# THE UNSEEN HAND OF GOD

I have known Ruth for forty years. Her story is so touching, so personal, I did not feel I should write it. I was convinced Ruth could do a better job than I would. Here is her testimony in her own words.

-------

My life began like a 1960s family sitcom. I had two parents who loved each other (and six brothers and sisters who tried to do the same), a nice house in the 'burbs, home-cooked meals every night, church on Sunday, and a loving mother sporting a dress and matching apron at home all day for us. My mom was an artist, full of talent. She made everything from scratch, including our clothes, and always had time for family craft projects and helping others in the community.

My father taught the Sunday Bible study at church. Dad worked for the Billy Graham Crusade. We had been steeped in God's Word and His love for us. And then the worst thing possible happened. Mom got sick. We watched her die of cancer. She was thirty-nine. I was ten. It felt to me like the act of a merciless and pitiless God.

There were no support groups back then. We went to school the following day, tried to be strong, and saved the grief for crying into our pillows at night. I personally was as mad as hell. Somehow I felt God was responsible and I was done with Him, even though I had witnessed a strong spiritual presence in my mother before she died. That presence of Christ was undeniable even as young as I was, and I have never forgotten it. But at the time it did not matter. Why my mother? She was the last person in the world who deserved that kind of suffering. She had done everything right and raised us to have faith. Mine was gone.

I proceeded to lash out in all the ways grieving kids do. I rebelled. I became self-destructive, combative, and grew a chip on my shoulder the size of the world. My poor father was also lost. This man who had never had to do so much as a load of laundry was now left to father seven grieving children all alone. My grandmothers stepped in to help. Being the one in the family who could not control her mouth, I went to battle with my dad. That resulted in my going to live with relatives.

I was later sent to a Christian boarding school across the country. Angry that I was now losing what supportive family and friends I still had, my intention was to run away when I arrived. I went to the orientation and plotted my runaway plan. But it was there that I met my soul sister Cindy. My plans changed.

Toward the end of the school year, Cindy invited me to spend the summer break with her parents on the west coast. I am pretty sure I said no, but she called her parents anyway, and they agreed to take me. God bless them forever. They had no clue what they were in for.

So began my journey through life and the many

struggles through which I passed, never realizing that I was very definitely under the unseen hand of God.

As we circled the airport of a beautiful beachside village, I saw a large throng of people holding a sign that read, "Welcome, Cindy and Ruth." As soon as we landed and stepped out of the airplane, we were enveloped by hugs and singing. I discovered that I would be living no more than a hundred yards from a beach on the Pacific Ocean. This, my new world, was populated by young college-age students with a love and enthusiasm for Christ that I had never seen nor could believe was real.

Any other teenager would have been full of gratitude for this opportunity in paradise, but not me. I was too full of being an angry victim and I was not letting it go.

We left the airport and headed for Cindy's home. I was aware that Cindy's father was a serious Christian. My expectation was that he would be wearing a black suit and had not smiled in decades.

Cindy's mother had driven us from the airport, and Cindy and I were in the backseat of the car. As we drove up the driveway, out came Cindy's dad. He walked over to the front of the car, and suddenly he turned into a mime. The mime decided to open the hood of the car and inspect it. As mimes do, he did some very funny things. He could not get the hood of the car open. All of this, of course, was played out in a totally imaginary state. The real hood would have opened, but the mime's hood would not open. The mime got his hand caught in the imaginary hood and could not get it out. Finally, in great agony, he freed that hand, only for the hood of the car to take captive his other hand. We could not help but laugh.

The mime finally was able to get the hood open. He stuck his head under the imaginary hood, only to have the hood fall on his head. The mime was very angry at the hood, but it nonetheless kept falling on him. By that time, we were in stitches. Suddenly the mime slammed his hood closed and made his way up onto the car. He did a little jig on the hood, climbed over the windshield to stand on top of the car, and danced another little jig. Eventually his feet showed up on Cindy's side. Then he turned to my side of the car and, lying flat on the roof, face at my window, he banged on the window and motioned for me to roll it down. Then, very soberly, very calmly, and in a way which was everyday naturalness, he said, "Hi, Ruth, welcome home."

I had never seen an introduction such as this, but that was only the beginning. I was living right in the middle of the "sixties." This little college town, which was one mile square, was the most rebellious, inordinate, and sinful square mile in the United States. During all the time I lived in that town, there was never a police car in that square mile where the college students lived because police would not enter that notorious square mile.

While I was there, the students burned down the bank. They had riots almost as though they were scheduled. At times when we would go off to school, every huge garbage bin in this little college community was blocking the roads. It was no small task to drive out of that village.

There, in the most sinful town imaginable, lived a group of more than one hundred Christians who were the most precious people I have ever known. They took care of my needs and loved me in ways I had never before been loved.

When the Christians gathered, they had meetings like nothing I had ever seen. Most of the meetings were either singing or sharing. As often as not, there was no planned speaker. Rather than a minister wearing a suit, there would be a brother, or sometimes even a sister, who would speak. Sometimes it would be Cindy's father.

We would march through the city arm in arm singing. Here was the closest thing to the first-century Christians that America will ever know. Even though there was probably never a town anywhere in the Western world quite as wild and untamed as was this one square mile of student housing, there were some of the most wonderful Christians, utterly untouched by their surroundings, almost as if the two worlds did not coexist.

Because we were at the Pacific Ocean, sometimes after a long evening meeting, we would walk down to the beach. There would be a half dozen to a dozen torches which would be planted into the sand, and a new convert would be baptized. All these hundred or more Christians would testify and exhort. Then the person about to be baptized would say something. If it was a young man being baptized, a man would baptize him. If it was a girl, a young Christian lady would baptize her.

One evening I was one of the people who was baptized. I was so happy at that time, but the pain I was holding onto with all my strength soon swallowed up the joy. How messed up must I have been that I could not even maintain a spiritual transformation surrounded by so much love and joy. It seemed at the time that even God's love could not save me from myself. I had such a wall up that even the strongest love could not get through, let alone happiness. I felt unworthy and ashamed and started to rebel against what few rules I even had left.

I look back on this and wonder how I could have withstood the love, the care, the joy, the meetings, and the presence of Christ and so much of His grace. Nonetheless, I managed to do just that. There I was, surrounded by more love than perhaps in any other place on earth. I was still in rebellion. My heart was still full of hate. I was determined that I would not love a God who would allow cancer to take my mother. There was an abundance of self-pity, as well as a sense of revenge against God and against the entire human race. How I could have mingled those two worlds together was inexplicable.

The hate was there, but there was also that unseen hand of God.

Then came the end of the summer and time to go back to the private school which I hated. Cindy would not be returning. After living in this place which belonged to another world, the thought of going back to that school provoked me to come up with a plot. When Cindy's mother drove me one hundred miles to the airport, I would tell her exactly how to get there. What Cindy's mother did not know was that I was going to give her wrong directions all the way. I was watching the time to make sure we would be lost long enough to miss my flight. Sure enough, we arrived at the airport far too late to be a passenger on that plane.

I began to cry. I said, "Cindy, call your father and talk to him. He will let me stay. Just call him. I know he will give his permission."

Sure enough, they found a phone and called Cindy's father. (This was before the time of cell phones.) Cindy's father knew full well what was in my heart. He knew that I was not going to behave and that I would be a continually difficult person to care for. Nonetheless, he said yes. It was not until later that I found out that he struggled very hard when he was asked to take me for another year. He capitulated, knowing that he was yielding to trouble and a great deal of it.

Cindy's mother turned the car around and drove us back one hundred miles to what would continue to be the most heavenly place any young girl could ever hope to live. Paradoxically, though I had a wonderful year there, my hatred of life returned. My rebellion would not die.

I was still having trouble with my family. I decided to run away from everyone. I was going to become an adult and let everyone know that I could take care of myself. I would not need my family, and I would not need God.

Some of my friends in that enchanted place gave me the address of their family who lived in Little Rock, Arkansas. I would be well received there.

I was at that time only sixteen years old; nonetheless, I was determined I would be an adult. I bought a train ticket from the West Coast to Little Rock. I had five dollars and an apple for the trip. I had no idea what the next month would hold.

I bought the ticket that would cross America, but there was one little problem. When I would reach San Antonio on my way to Arkansas, there would be a one-and-a-half-day layover. I planned to stay in what I imagined to be a large train station and move around for a day and a half without being noticed until I could continue on to

Arkansas. I could not have been more wrong in what I imagined awaited me.

My trip to San Antonio should have been an absolute, total disaster. I had no money for food or drink, but I did not understand the ways of the Lord. Once more, out of the graces of God, there came that unseen hand, which would take me to San Antonio, shield me from all possible harm, and take me safely to Little Rock.

How did I buy a ticket? I was too young for a driver's license. For ID I took some junk mail from a girl who had moved and made the train reservation under her name. I did that so no one could find me.

When I got to the Amtrak counter to claim my ticket, they asked for my ID. I explained that I did not have my license yet, but I had some mail with my name on it. Would that work? And it did!

I was reminded by the Amtrak agent that I would have a long layover in San Antonio. At that time, I was given a seating assignment and told exactly where I would find my seat. Once more, by the hand of God, I was seated beside a passenger whose name was Bea. Bea was traveling with her mother, but my seat was beside Bea.

What I did not know was that Bea was actually an angel sent directly by the Lord to watch over this sixteen-year-old blonde runaway. I have never forgotten, nor will I ever forget, Bea.

Bea noticed that I was not eating anything. She invited me to the dining car. I kept wanting to go, but I only had five dollars. What if everything on the menu cost more than five dollars? Bea or others might realize that I was not only a runaway, but that I had no money. When Bea persisted, I explained that I really was not hungry. This did not deter Bea. When she came back from the dining car, she always brought food for me. She explained that she had some food left over that she could not eat and asked if I would eat the rest of it so it would not be wasted.

As we approached San Antonio, Bea asked me where I would be staying during the day-and-a-half layover. By now I knew that Bea was wise. The question was: What would Bea do? Would she turn me over to the police as a runaway? What else might she do?

Around midnight I saw two of the Amtrak agents coming down the aisle. I was certain that Bea had turned me in. The two agents bent down beside my seat.

I knew it was all over. They explained in a whisper that they were trying not to alert the other passengers, but they and the rest of the crew had taken up a donation to make sure that I would be safe all the way to my final destination.

Again, there was that persistent hand of God on a sixteen-year-old runaway.

Asking no questions, the agents slipped a wad of money into my hand and walked away. I was stunned! I remember sitting there, trying to wrap my head around what had just happened. I also remember looking over at Bea, who was pretending to sleep, and I felt the spirit of my mother.

The next morning, the engineer, along with another member of the crew, came to my seat and asked me to come with them to the rear car. Again, I felt that I had been found out and would surely be collected by the police when we arrived in San Antonio.

I sat down in the engineer's office. He explained that he wanted Bea to be there as a witness to what was about to happen. The engineer asked absolutely nothing about my situation. He explained that he lived in San Antonio and would be getting off the train and going to his home to be with his family that night. He said to me, "If you have nowhere to stay during the layover in San Antonio, you are welcome to come and stay with my family."

Using an Amtrak telephone, the engineer connected me with his wife. She explained to me that they had two daughters who were away at school and that I was more than welcome to spend the night there in the bedroom of their daughters.

The engineer told me that before he could go home, he would have a great deal of paperwork to do and that I should stay in the train station until he was free to go home. When I walked into the train station, I was shocked. The train station was small. Furthermore, the station was out in the country. There was no one else around except me. Everything looked scary. Outside there were only two rough-looking men who were sitting there drinking beer and talking. I was overwhelmed at the thought of having to spend the night there. This was an extremely dangerous place for a young girl to be.

I was about to say goodbye to Bea. At that point, she handed me an envelope with fifteen dollars. Ten dollars of that money was from Bea; five dollars was from her mother. I protested, but both refused to take the money back. I would say that at that point, I had a God and some angels who were very, very busy taking care of a frightened young girl.

In tears I tried to give the money back again, but Bea stuffed it back into my hand and hugged me goodbye with what I believe was a prayer in Spanish.

The engineer gave me a tour of the city on the way to his home. We arrived and I met his wife, a wonderful woman. She was preparing a barbecue in the backyard for a gathering, which would take place that evening. This wonderful lady showed me to the room where I would stay. She told me to take a shower if I so desired and to take a nap if I needed one.

So it was that I found housing better than any motel I could have imagined. I showered and fell asleep. I woke up to the smell of barbecue, which had never smelled so good.

Their guests arrived; they were part of their family. Not one soul questioned me about anything. All they did was make me feel at home. I had to fight back tears. The Lord's presence looking after me never departed. Once more, that hand!

The next morning, the engineer took me back to the train station. Then he left. He had slipped something into my pocket. I took my seat on the train and reached into my pocket to find whatever it was the engineer had given me. It was money, and it was also the telephone number of the engineer and his wonderful wife.

The train pulled out of the station bound for Little Rock, Arkansas. There was not an angel, but a band of angels, who were taking care of a runaway.

In Little Rock, I would be the guest of relatives of my friends in the town in which I had lived the previous couple of years. These people worked for a television station in Little Rock. They had managed to get me an internship with the TV station. The job was waiting for me when I arrived.

In the next few days, I learned how to set up a television camera. I was to haul gear whenever it was needed and to make coffee for the entire crew.

I called my sister, whom I was missing a great deal, and explained the situation. I added, "Tell Dad that I am here in Arkansas and that I am not leaving until he gives me permission to be on my own."

My sister conveyed the message from my dad. He

agreed that I could return to the West Coast and stay there permanently. I would not have to go back to the private school. He agreed that I could be emancipated, but he added, "If you want to be an adult, then be one; I am not giving you any money to get from Little Rock to the West Coast."

The very next day was my first day to work out in the field with the crew of the television station. What they would be doing that day was to cover the horse races in Hot Springs, Arkansas. I set up the cameras, and with nothing else to do, I decided to go meet the horses. I need to explain that I had on a jacket that identified me as an employee of the television station. Otherwise, I could not have done what I was about to do, because I was a minor.

After visiting the horses, I wandered over to the bidding window area. There I met two old-timers who taught me the art of betting on horses. Against everything the old-timers had just taught me, I placed all the cash I had on me, which was three dollars, on the friendliest horse I had met. I did know that because of my age, I was doing something illegal.

If you find the next words hard to believe, so do I.

I never looked at the odds board. I did not know that I had picked the horse that was the longshot of the entire day. I had picked him only because he was friendly.

As incredible as it may seem, he not only placed; he won! The three dollars that I placed on a nag had come in first with the highest odds that could be placed on a horse.

There I was with three dollars, but now I suddenly had enough money to buy a plane ticket back to the West Coast *and* to buy lunch for the television crew. Did that friendly horse go out of his way to come in as the winner just for me?

I was beginning to think that just perhaps the Lord had not forgotten me, despite all my rebellion and the few rules by which I lived, all of which I had broken. It is hard not to believe that the Lord Himself was taking care of me. That day the unseen hand of God was not particularly unseen.

The reason it was urgent for me to return to the West Coast was that the next week I was to take an efficiency examination which would allow me to graduate from high school a year early.

I got on a plane and flew back to the West Coast.

Cindy and her parents greeted me with open arms, all three of them totally ignoring what I had done and treating me as though none of this had ever happened.

Later I began to reflect on all the people I had hurt since my mother's death. I had caused so many people so much grief. I had failed so many friends and my family. Was there not a way to stop me from bringing so much sadness, hurt, and disappointment into the lives of other people?

I eventually shut everyone out, including my father, and went to live by myself. Being alone would ensure that no one could leave me again, nor would I hurt anyone anymore. Further, I would show my father that I did not need anyone. But the reality of having to live by myself was beyond depressing. I crashed and burned.

Even though I had finished school, was holding down a good job, and was supporting myself, I was, nonetheless, still wallowing in anger. I was a miserable, unhappy mess. Sadness enveloped me. I was tired—tired of being miserable and wondering why I could not find happiness somewhere in all my bitterness and anger.

I was now eighteen years old and had so little to show for it. It was also that same year that my grandmother, who was so much like my mother, passed away. It was more than I could bear. I gave up. A thought was beginning to take possession of me. Somehow I convinced myself that everyone would be much better off without my problems in their lives, and the best thing I could do for them was to end my life.

I did not let anyone know that I was considering taking my life. I had rejected every act of love I had been given, and the self-loathing and sadness were drowning me. Carrying around a lifetime of anger had worn me down. I wanted my mom.

I planned to make certain that there was no way for me to survive what I was about to do. I took a medication that I knew was deadly and then doubled the dosage. (I took twice as much of this medicine as Marilyn Monroe had taken many years earlier.) I passed out with the final thought that I would never regain consciousness. I would die and just possibly might see my mother again.

I would like to tell you what happened next. The poison I took was so deadly, I did not recover by simply opening my eyes and finding out that I was alive. I opened my eyes, but my thoughts had little awareness to them. The only thing I knew was that there was a window. I kept looking at the window, trying to understand what that window was and what it meant to me. Little by little, I began to recollect a few thoughts and some memories, but it would be a long, long rehabilitation to bring me back to the day when I would be in the land of the living.

I vaguely remembered an ambulance. I remembered a man was beating on my chest and swearing profusely. He was screaming at me. I had the feeling later that whoever that man was, there was a time in his life when he had lost someone he was trying to save. I feel as though he was saying to himself, "I am not going to lose another one! This young girl is not going to die. I am not going to let her die."

I was in a hospital room when I became conscious that there was a nurse in the room. When I opened my eyes, she came to my bedside and asked me a few questions. Then she literally ran out of the room in search of a doctor.

What happened next was that I scanned the room wondering, "Am I alive?" I could neither speak nor move. I was gradually becoming aware that I had not died but was coming back to the conscious world.

Soon a team of doctors surrounded my bed, asking if I understood them. They told me they had no explanation for why I was alive. In theory, I could not possibly be alive. They had done the toxicology, and I had done my homework. I clearly should not be alive. The doctors knew as well as I did that no one could swallow that much poison and live.

One of the doctors explained, "We are men of science, yet we can offer no explanation for why you are alive."

Another doctor asked me, "Do you believe in God? If not, you should reconsider, because the cognitive and neurological damage should have turned you into a vegetable."

It is true that it took me several years to fully recover while I learned to walk and speak.

As I recovered, everything seemed new and brilliant. Colors, fabrics, the sky . . . there was a magical wonderment about everything. I was seeing everything with new eyes and a new spirit. The reality that God had saved me was undeniable and was with me constantly. Peace was now mine.

Other changes to my life were on the way. While I

was living in that college community, I had had a roommate named Marilyn. Of all the wonderful Christians in that gathering, the one who stood out the most to me was my roommate. Marilyn came to visit me in the hospital frequently. She was there on the day I was discharged.

I was several years younger than Marilyn. She let me know that she was adopting me. That is, she would be with me every step of the way in my new life. She was teaching a class in self-esteem at the junior college in our town. She told them that I would be attending the class. In the class, she said to me, along with others, "I want you to repeat these words: I am an important person. I am worthy."

Those were the last words on earth I wanted to use to describe myself. I started to get up and go out of the room, but Marilyn stopped me, pushed me back in the chair, and said, "Leaving this room is not an option."

In the coming weeks, Marilyn taught me to understand several things. One was that I had taught myself to react negatively and with anger to any input. This was the world I had created and in which I had lived since the day my mother died. Marilyn helped me to realize that I did not have to be a self-made victim for the rest of my life. She helped me to see that I had every reason to be angry and sad about the death of my mother, but I did not need to wear it like a millstone around my neck.

Somehow I had felt that if I accepted my mother's death, it would mean that I did not care about her. It had never occurred to me that I could accept my mother's death, let the anger go, and move on with the strength and love that my mother would have wanted.

As I reflect on the pivotal role that Marilyn played in my life, I want to say to you, my reader, that Marilyn is the closest to a saint that we Protestants will ever have.

Marilyn is no longer with us, but her memory is still with me.

[*Reader, Ruth and I agreed that, at this point, we would like to dedicate this story to Marilyn for a life lived wholly for the Lord.*]

As my new view of life became part of my daily living, I started working as a volunteer with people whose task was preventing others from committing suicide. So radical was the change in my life that the one who needed help was now giving help.

Perhaps most drastically different of all, I am now

leading a happy life. The conditions of life have not changed: there is still disappointment, abandonment, problems, and situations identical to what I had been through earlier. But! In those same kinds of negative situations, I now remain in peace, full of gratitude for what I have. I could allow those same events to bury me, or I can choose to respond to all the circumstances in my life by giving them a silver lining and responding positively to everything which I had previously given a negative response.

You will find me saying to people who are on the brink of suicide: "No matter how bad your situation has become or how helpless you feel, you can make a choice to respond positively. Letting everything that comes into your life be negative must go. It is possible for you to grow from the terrible situations you have passed through in your life. Finding something positive in whatever is taking place in your life is the beginning step to gradually having eyes to discover worth and value in the circumstances through which you are passing. You have everything you need to have a good life, despite all of the circumstances which life brings.

I repeat what a doctor said to me when I was in

the hospital and could hardly understand his words: "If you do not believe in God, you might want to consider it now."

<hr />

Today Ruth is in her midfifties. I see her from time to time. I remember her when she was fourteen and fifteen. It is only her name and her physical appearance that have remained the same. You cannot bring Ruth down, not by any circumstances on this earth. She is always cheerful, loving, and appreciative. I also learned something else. She can certainly write her testimony. I am not ashamed to say to you, Ruth, I do not think I have ever seen anyone who is not a professional writer express their life's journey so beautifully and perfectly as you have.

The last time I saw Ruth, she spoke of the unseen hand of God that had followed her throughout her life. I agreed.

She said, "It was the unseen hand of God then and it still is!"

It would be wonderful if many Christians could

hear Ruth give her testimony. What she was and what she is today are two different people. Today Ruth is a masterpiece of God's grace. It was the unseen hand of God that has been in her life with a purpose as beautiful and as great as was the suffering and the sorrow. God allows situations to come into our lives which He hates in order to bring to pass things which He loves.

# CHAPTER 22

# WHAT THE STUNNED SURGEONS FOUND IN THE OPERATING ROOM

It was July the Fourth. Annie had expended a great deal of energy celebrating with her family that day. Evening arrived and going to bed was inviting to all. In the middle of the night, Annie's twelve-year-old daughter, Marie, came to her mother's bedside complaining that her chest hurt and she couldn't breathe well. After calming Marie, Annie decided she could wait until morning to take Marie to the family doctor.

So it was, Annie and her daughter were soon explaining the events of the night before to the family doctor. He asked a series of questions and listened to Marie's heart and lungs. The doctor finally concluded, "I do not think we have any serious problem here. I believe it is asthma. I will call in a prescription for an inhaler. Just in case though, I have ordered a chest X-ray."

After the X-ray was taken, the mother and daughter went to the pharmacy to pick up the prescription for the inhaler. While there, the pharmacist told Annie, "There is a call for you, Annie."

It was the doctor's office trying to reach her, and one of the doctor's staff told Annie, "Get to the hospital immediately. The doctor will be there waiting for you."

Annie immediately called her husband and repeated the doctor's words to him. She and Marie got in the car, and Annie stopped for nothing. A few minutes later mother and daughter were at the hospital.

The doctor reported that the X-ray had revealed an enlarged heart. Over the next several hours there were blood tests taken, then came an MRI, then more tests. Finally, Annie and her husband were called into a small room with a table and three chairs. The doctor gave his diagnosis. His words, so unexpected, were: "The tests show us your daughter not only has an enlarged heart," the doctor paused, "tests reveal that she has lymphoma. Further, it appears the lymphoma has spread to her heart. This is very unusual."

The operations would take two sessions. A cardiac surgeon would operate first. When he finished, he would turn Marie over to the thoracic surgeon to complete the exploration of cancer. He would also insert a port for chemotherapy, and chemotherapy would begin the next day.

All of this news was received on Thursday. Marie would have surgery Monday morning. Marie was sent home on Friday with the suggestion to go home and enjoy the weekend.

In disbelief, Annie repeated the words back to the doctor. "My daughter has an enlarged heart. She has cancer. She will have surgery Monday morning. Did I hear you say, 'Have a good weekend?'"

After leaving the hospital, Annie went straight to the nearest phone. She called her pastor. He alerted the rest of the church staff, who in turn contacted a group of men and women whose responsibility was to notify the congregation of prayer requests. In a short time, many people knew of Marie's surgery scheduled for Monday and began praying for her. By Monday morning, the Lord had heard many prayers for Marie.

Something else happened on the day Annie heard the state of Marie's health. Finding herself alone with her thoughts and in a puddle of tears, Annie cried to the Lord: "Lord, thank you for Marie. She is such a good girl. I love her with all my heart and soul. I know she is Yours, she has always been Yours. She is Yours now. I am giving her to You. She is completely in Your hands. She is Yours to do whatever it is You decide to do. I ask—I beg—for Your divine healing, but whatever Your will, I will find a way to live with it."

Making it through the weekend was not easy for Annie nor anyone else in the family. Yet, they were strong for Marie, so she would not be more frightened than she already was. Annie and her husband were fearful of Monday and what it would bring. Their one comfort was knowing prayers from around the country were being offered for their daughter.

Early Monday morning, with many Christians praying and with Marie's life completely turned over to the Lord, Marie was taken to the operating room.

After what seemed to be an interminable time, the cardiac surgeon came to Annie and her husband.

"I do not know what to say. I can only tell you this: I have held Marie's heart in my hands, and her heart is completely normal. It is perfectly well. I have seen the X-rays and the MRI, both showing an enlarged heart with shadows on it."

The surgeon struggled for a moment.

"Nonetheless, Marie's heart is fine. The thoracic surgeon is working on her right now. You will not be able to see her until she is awake and in recovery. Good luck."

So began the second vigil.

A highly experienced surgical staff worked on Marie for what seemed once more like an eternity. Annie and her husband found themselves waiting for news that would almost certainly be the difference between life and death for their little girl.

The hours passed. Knowing that the two of them would not be able to see Marie until she was in that recovery room was almost unbearable.

Finally, a nurse found Annie and her husband.

"We would like to ask the two of you to come into the operating room where your daughter is. Marie is not awake yet; still, the doctor and the surgical team would like to speak with you. Would you please come with me."

Annie and her husband looked at each other, again realizing that the news they were about to hear would not be good: that the tests had shown cancer. Marie was not awake. They were supposed to see her in the recovery room; instead, they were being invited into the surgical room. Nobody is allowed in an operating room. Had Marie died?

Annie took a deep breath and remembered her prayer of surrender.

When Annie and her husband entered the operating room, the entire surgical team was standing in a circle around Marie. The surgeon spoke.

"I have seen all the test results on your daughter. There was no question that your daughter had cancer. We have no explanation, but this morning your daughter Marie has no cancer. Your daughter is fine."

He repeated himself, "There is no cancer. We see no cancer, and her heart is not enlarged. Marie is perfectly normal. As a precaution, we have taken a biopsy, but I can, with almost certainty, tell you that with my years of experience of seeing cancer in patients, there is no cancer in Marie. What we see here today has absolutely no explanation."

One totally impossible miracle! But two?

Upon receiving this unexpected news, Annie, almost falling to her knees, began to cry. The surgical team that encircled Marie assured them that this was an unprecedented event. Their eyes moved from Marie to Annie and her husband, then back to Marie. The news that was being delivered by the surgeon obviously brought great emotion with it to everyone in that room. No one had any explanation for what all were witnessing. After all, that many blood tests, MRIs, and X-rays could not have been wrong! Annie knew the explanation: It was a miracle from God. He had saved Marie.

After several weeks of painful recuperation from the exploratory surgery, Marie returned to school and normal activities. She never asked, "Why me?"

As she grew up and graduated college, she considered having plastic surgery to remove the huge scar that remained from the operation. After careful consideration, she determined that scar is a part of who she is, a part of her journey, and a reminder of the miracle she is.

If you were to talk to Annie today, she would tell you, had it not been for a miracle straight from the hand of God, it might have gone the other way, with Marie having cancer, heart issues, and possibly not living through it.

This beautiful girl, who today is in her thirties, so far has lived a highly athletic, adventurous, sometimes even physically daring life.

There is a term that the scientific world finally had to come up with. That term is *spontaneous remission*. The Christians in Annie's church have another term for it: a divine miracle, inexplicable to man but totally understood by those who believe.

Miracles are the undeserved gift of God coming from the overflowing grace of our Lord and Savior Jesus Christ.

# CHAPTER 23

# THE MYSTERY OF
# DA VINCI'S *LAST SUPPER*

It is an exciting thing to feel your train move into the station at Milan and to know that in just a few moments you will be on your way to the convent of St. Mary of Grace, where Leonardo da Vinci's masterpiece *The Last Supper* is housed.

Leonardo da Vinci was born out of wedlock in the town of Vinci, Italy. Something happened in the union of genetics of the man and woman who produced a genius with nondimensional sight who seemed to peer into the future and see things others could not imagine.

In the sketches of his notebooks, you will find the perfect drawing of a bicycle—which did not yet exist—a helicopter, an airplane, a parachute, and even the concept of a submarine. He advanced the world of weapon-making. He was an engineer, an artist, a sculptor, and a painter. Every generation has been intrigued by the mind of Leonardo da Vinci.

Da Vinci is often considered the most brilliant visionary who ever lived. An illustration of the difference between the workings of the mind of da Vinci and the minds of most of us can be illustrated by the difference between an inchworm and a grasshopper. Most people's brains work like an inchworm. We make progress one step at a time as we move forward in our thinking. But there have been a few people born with a mind that we might compare to the grasshopper. They do not come to a problem and inch their way through little by little, step by step. Rather, like the grasshopper, they see things in wholes, jump across the available information, and come to a conclusion, sometimes instantly.

The mind most common to us is called the linear mind, always moving in one line, following a reasonable cognition. The other is called a spherical mind. The spherical mind can take in whole concepts and, having seen from one end to the other and everything in between, come to a conclusion. At the very least, a person with a spherical mind is seen as someone who can synthesize many different portions of knowledge, which would appear to others as unrelated, put them together, and come forth with a conclusion no one else has ever seen before.

In a world where virtually everyone has a linear mind, the spherical mind, at the very least, can often be misunderstood. Leonardo da Vinci, possibly the most intelligent man who has ever lived, had a spherical mind. An estimate of his IQ is 200—off the charts.

Da Vinci had many successes, but he also had many failures and disappointments. He worked on a lead and ceramic horse for more than ten years. When war broke out between city-states, his work of a lifetime was melted down to use the lead for bullets.

Da Vinci is known as an Italian, but he died in France. I visited the castle in the Loire Valley in France where the famous two intertwining staircases come up to the room where he died. I was given the privilege of being in that room alone for about half an hour while I thought over this great man's life, including his wonderful rendition of *The Last Supper*.

There are many stories which are not widely known about da Vinci and *The Last Supper*. The most intriguing to me is a choice da Vinci made about one of the models chosen to pose as one of the thirteen men who appear in the finished work.

The room where *The Last Supper* was painted was a galley, or a dining room, for people who worked in the convent of St. Mary of Grace. This galley jutted up against a stone hill. Just how would Leonardo da Vinci take a stone wall and turn it into a "canvas" upon which to paint *The Last Supper*? First, he covered the stone with one layer of plaster, and then a second layer, until he had a smooth surface. Then he introduced a brilliantly white lead-based paint, which would be used in a few places to depict light shining through the windows he would depict in *The Last Supper*. The rest of the now flat, smooth surface was covered with acrylic. Unfortunately, that particular mix of acrylic was a concoction of Leonardo da Vinci's that would not endure the ravages of time.

Da Vinci did not know that in the first century people would lie down and brace themselves on their left arms while they ate with their right hands. Not knowing this, da Vinci sketched the table. There would be thirteen people seated at the table. Jesus would be in the center. There would be six men on one side of Him and six men on the other. The men were arranged in groups of three . . . two groups of three on Jesus' left and two groups of three on His right.

The first figure he chose to paint was that of Jesus. The time had come for Leonardo da Vinci to find someone in the city of Milan to pose for the face of Christ. Our famous artist did not take this task lightly. He visited cathedrals and monasteries. He watched people coming into and leaving Mass. He was looking for a kind, gentle face that emitted a holy countenance. At last he made his choice. He approached the young man and explained that he was looking for someone to pose as a model for the central face of his work. The man agreed. So began *The Last Supper*.

The man who posed for the face of Jesus was escorted into a very small room, something which could be compared to a small dining room. There was nothing on the wall at all. When his task serving as a model was finished and he departed, he saw nothing on the wall except the figure of one person—Jesus. The rest of the wall was empty.

We know from his notes and sketches that da Vinci planned to paint *The Last Supper* depicting the very moment when Jesus said, "One of you will betray me." Each of the twelve apostles would show their surprise and wonderment as to which one of them would actually betray Him.

Once the figure of Jesus was completed, da Vinci labored over painting the eleven apostles for the next three years. Each distinctive face and figure would be in a unique position, each of them asking, "Which one of us will betray the Lord?"

At the end of those three years, everything was finished except for the face and figure of Judas. Da Vinci set out to find the most wicked face in all of Milan to pose for the face of Judas. This time he did not go to the Catholic Mass, nor to the monasteries, but to the most dangerous parts of the city, always looking for the most wretched face his eyes might behold. He went to the jails and the prisons, seeking the most depraved criminals of the city for the face etched with the highest degree of debauchery.

Finally, da Vinci made his choice. The man was a criminal and an ex-prisoner. He was a man who filled his life with depravity.

Da Vinci approached the man.

"I would like you to pose for me. I have almost completed a large mural in the convent of St. Mary of Grace. When I have finished this figure, my work will be completed."

The man agreed.

Soon the man was following da Vinci through the monastery into the small dining room. For a moment, the man stood transfixed. He realized that he had been in this room before. It was three years earlier when there was nothing upon that wall except the kind and gentle face of Jesus. Now he saw the nearly completed mural. There was nothing lacking except the face of one man.

The man looked at the body which had already been painted. The hands of the figure were clutching a bag holding the twenty pieces of silver given to the man who would betray Jesus Christ. There was also a small bowl of salt, which had been turned over. In the culture of the day, of which the artist was familiar, spilled salt was a sign that the servant would betray his master.

Suddenly, the man brought in to pose clutched his head and screamed. Those in the room, including da Vinci, were startled. The man pointed toward the painting of Jesus.

"Three years ago, I entered this room with you. You asked me to pose as a model for the face of Jesus Christ. Now, three years later, you are asking me to portray the face of Judas!"

Such was the mystery of da Vinci's *Last Supper.* A man with such an angelic face had so given his life to debauchery, depravity, and things of the flesh that his very countenance, the very skin on his face, now announced the evil of his heart.

It was no less than Napoleon who made the observation that by the time a man is very old, what he has become is etched on his face. This man, however, had so lived his life that it had not taken a lifetime, but only three years. The face of innocence and purity was now imprinted with all the debauchery of Milan. It is not easy for a man to give himself so completely to darkness that his face, which once portrayed the kindness of Christ, now portrayed the face of Judas.

By the time of Leonardo da Vinci's death in 1517,

the oil painting was already cracking and flaking. Less than fifty years later, da Vinci's *Last Supper* was in ruins. Nonetheless, some of those flakes had been saved. There had been many restorations, all of which had failed. Then in the year 1980, there was a new commission issued for total restoration. By careful study of the room, the wall, the flakes, the X-rays, and other scientific means, they were able to discern the colors used in the original painting. Science has brought back to us da Vinci's masterpiece, his secrets of lighting, color, and the knowledge of its original appearance.

The restoration took twenty years, and it was open to the public in 1999. The paint was chosen for its durability. The room itself has been insulated; a dehumidifier is hard at work in that room twenty-four hours a day. No matter how few or how many people are in this small room—no more than approximately twenty people are allowed in the room at the same time—delicate instruments measure the heat and humidity. The temperature of seventy degrees never changes.

The painting today is an exact replica of da Vinci's original work. The startled faces are asking one another the ultimate question, "Who will betray the Christ?"

and the bag of silver coins are evident in the hand of Judas. Some say they can see a similarity in the faces of Jesus and Judas; others cannot. This restoration, unlike the original which lasted only a few years, should remain as it is for several hundred years.

Let the scream of the criminal never be forgotten, nor how a man's entire countenance can change in three short years simply by the way he lives his life on earth.

# CHAPTER 24

# NOT BY WORDS,
# NOT BY DEEDS

How can I, how can anyone, tell you about Beta? It was not by any word nor any deed Beta ever said or did that can explain her influence on my Christian walk.

I met Beta after I heard of a group of believers in Louisville, Kentucky, who met in homes. They were the only people who met in a living room for church any- where in the country that I knew of at that time. I was thirty-one. Beta, a former missionary to China, was seventy-one. Beta had been a member of the Little Flock of China. She had lived in Shanghai under the ministry of Watchman Nee. I came to learn she had been imprisoned by the Japanese in China at the outbreak of World War II.

Few Americans were privileged to ever meet or come to know Beta. Those who did know her agree that we had met one of the greatest Christians we would ever meet in our lifetimes.

The first time I met Beta, I simply asked her, "Tell me your story."

As Beta spoke, I was aware I was hearing something that I had never known of before. I was very quiet.

Suddenly she broke in with a question: "Would you like for me to stop?"

I had not uttered a sound; I had not moved while she spoke. I replied almost in a whisper, "Ma'am, do not stop under any circumstances whatsoever. I am listening with everything I have."

And so I heard her story.

Beta had been raised in a devout family. As a single woman at the age of twenty-two, she went to China under the auspices of the Methodist church. She lived in China, learned the Chinese language, and set about being a missionary.

There at the Methodist compound she met a young Chinese man who was somewhat shallow and uninspiring. Later this man spent some time meeting with the Little Flock. Beta knew that the Little Flock was a very controversial Christian movement in China, not having the wonderful reputation that it has today. When the young man returned to the Methodist compound, Beta noticed that he was a totally transformed person and that when he spoke, he spoke with a depth and strength that she had never heard before.

Beta continued. "I decided to go to Shanghai to visit the Little Flock. I also had a question that no one seemed to have an answer for."

She arrived in Shanghai, went to the place where the church gathered, and asked permission to meet Watchman Nee and ask him a question. She sat down and waited a moment for him to appear. He walked over, took a chair right in front of her, and said, "I understand you have a question you would like to ask."

For about twenty minutes Beta struggled to try to explain that she did not understand head covering.

When she finished, Nee, as was typical of him, answered with one sentence: "I would to God that I could wear a thousand head coverings for Christ."

He rose and left the room.

Beta decided to stay and get to know these controversial Christians who found no need of any help from the Western world or from missionaries.

"After several days, I decided to become part of the Little Flock. I returned to the mission compound and wrote a letter to the Methodist mission and to the people who supported me from Kentucky."

Her letter contained a request: "Please do not send any more money to me. I am going to live here among the Chinese Christians, and I will find some means of my own support."

Beta continued her story, but it was not anything she said that so profoundly moved me. It was the presence of Christ in her life.

<hr>

There was a special dinner and a meeting planned for that evening to welcome this new guest who had arrived from Texas. I stepped out and sat down on the back porch. What could cause me, sitting on a porch, to experience one of the most memorable moments of my entire life? It was watching Beta Scheirich swing a little three-year-old on a children's swing. Beta was at least twenty feet from me, but I was overwhelmed with the presence of the Lord.

No one had ever accused Beta of being beautiful. She was six feet tall and gangly. That did not bother her one bit.

I have lived many years and have traveled the world. I have known ministers, literally thousands, and worked very closely with many of them, but never in all my life have I ever met anyone with whom I felt the presence of the Lord just by being near them.

Nor is that just my testimony; it's the testimony of others who came to know Beta as well. I was never in the presence of Beta when I was not in the presence of the Lord. I know of no great thing Beta ever accomplished. I cannot specifically remember a sentence she ever said to me. Yet, until this day she remains the greatest spiritual influence on my life other than Christ Himself. Not by word, not by deed.

I must now finish the story of what happened to Beta in China.

Beta was not the only missionary who had become part of the Little Flock. There was Mary Jones of Wales; a lady named Rademacher; and Miss Fishbacher of England who was a master not only of English but also Chinese. Miss Fishbacher helped Watchman Nee with many of his books, which were basically messages he brought, with the exception of his book entitled *Our Missions*, which he wrote out by hand.

There came a radical change in China on December 8, 1941. Upon that day, simultaneously the Japanese began to invade the Philippines, Singapore, the coastal region of China, and Guam.

Within a few weeks Shanghai had been taken over completely by the Japanese.

Some of the foreigners fled; others decided to stay. After a few more weeks, Beta and the other women whom I mentioned were ordered to come to the train station to be taken to an internment camp.

Beta explained to me with great emotion that Watchman Nee, under great risk to his own life, accompanied them all to the train station where the Japanese glared at him but did not arrest him.

Part of the story of Beta's experience in that concentration camp, which she told me in detail, was getting one meal per day consisting of a piece of bread and some soup. Beta recounted that everyone closed their eyes while they ate the soup, certain that they did not want to see what it was they were eating. Some of the stories about the food and about the conditions of the camp were so graphic that I will not repeat them here.

This story, dear reader, even today is not easy for me to tell.

Japan was at war with America. Americans who were captured were treated terribly. The Japanese were very proud that they were never willing to ever be taken prisoners. (They would die rather than surrender; therefore, anyone who did surrender, no matter what nationality, was considered a coward unworthy of any consideration.) The Japanese realized that there were Japanese who had been living in America, working at the Japanese Embassy, who had been taken to concentration camps. The Japanese in American camps were treated very well. Not so for the Westerners who were in Japanese concentration camps.

The Swedish Embassy made arrangements for Americans who were prisoners of the Japanese, and Japanese who were prisoners of the Americans, to be exchanged. After many months and many false reports, the exchange began. A Japanese ship sailed to India with Americans on board, including Beta; a neutral ship disembarked from America bringing the Japanese. The two ships would meet somewhere near the Cape of Good Hope. There the Americans would leave the Japanese ship and board the neutral ship, and the Japanese would disembark from the neutral ship and would board the Japanese ship. The Japanese ship would then turn around and go back to Japan and the neutral ship of Swedish origin would turn around and take the former American prisoners to a port in New Jersey.

One of the most touching stories of World War II, which has been almost totally forgotten, was the arrival of the ship named the MS *Gripsholm* in the American harbor. It had taken a total of four months at sea for the exchange to be completed. As the ship came closer to American shores, tugboats from the east coast came into the harbor to greet the ship, as well as hundreds of thousands of spectators. Many of the tugs sprayed an arch of water over the ship. Sirens sounded while ships blew their whistles and blasted their horns.

Beta had returned to America. The year was 1943.

She began to pray for workers who would be indigenous to America, who would raise up nontraditional churches here in the United States. This would be the burden she would carry until the day she died.

That statement begs for an explanation. The United States is less than three hundred years old. Its culture is not American. The culture that we have was brought here from Great Britain. Beta knew wisely something most of us did not understand: there had never been a clearly American expression of church. How she could know that is a mystery.

The only way we would ever know a truly American expression of the church would be if it grew up out of the soil of this land, a spontaneous, organic expression of His body. Spontaneous and organic are thoughts with which we were not particularly familiar. Beta had witnessed a spontaneous and organic church in China wholly outside the practices of the Western way of doing church.

Some people have called Beta an intercessor. That is not a term that fits Beta. No, Beta was not an intercessor; what made Beta so unusual was her capacity to simply sit in the presence of her Lord.

There was one other element. It was suffering. Not suffering which we put up with or tolerate, or perhaps even at which we rebel, but an acquiescence to pain, to suffering, and to rejection.

Out of humility, Beta usually ended up as the guest who cooked, or the person who volunteered to do child care. As a result, most people did not recognize who Beta really was.

Soon after I met Beta, I went to a conference in New York City. Some other young men and I stayed after the meetings to pray. I was down on my knees asking the Lord to break me beyond any mercy or any circumstance. What I did not know was that Beta was present in that room. It was at that time that Beta began to lift my name up to the Lord.

That very same summer I contracted a very deadly, incurable disease.

For years I did not see Beta. One day she came to visit me. I was too sick to get out of bed. It was then, on that last time I saw her, that she informed me she had sat terrified at the conference in New York City, hearing the prayers I had prayed for the Lord to break me, and from that time on she had brought me specifically before the Lord every day.

About two years later I gradually began to recover from that disease. Unfortunately, it was also about this same season that Beta died. She was seventy-seven. When I heard of Beta's death, I uttered three words spontaneously: "*It is time*. It's time, Lord."

I often wonder this: In a realm which has no time, where there is no past or future, have Beta's prayers for me finished? Or in that timeless realm, is Beta still praying for me?

If she is, then I am one of the most blessed and honored of men.

This woman has influenced my spiritual life more than all else combined; yet not with words, not with deeds, but because of the overwhelming presence of Christ pouring out of her life. This is how Beta influenced my life.

There are not many days since her death that I have not remembered Beta. Not one sentence did she ever utter to me that was a life changer or even memorable. Not by words, not by deeds, but by His presence.

Beta, I will see you again, in a place with which you are so familiar, lost in the presence of your Lord.

# CHAPTER 25

# A SECOND PAUL
# OF TARSUS

The greatest Christian man I have ever known was Prem Pradhan of Nepal. The life he lived ranks head and shoulders above any life story I have ever heard. In suffering, in persecution, in ministry, and in the planting of churches under grievous circumstances, to find his equal we have to go all the way back through church history until we come to Paul.

You need only read 2 Corinthians 6 and 11 to know the story of Prem Pradhan's life. For years Prem was my closest friend. It was also my privilege, on occasion, to cowork with him.

If anyone should ever wonder about Prem Pradhan's testimony, let me offer you a challenge. See if you can find anyone who has the scars of fetters—chains and shackles—around both wrists and ankles. If you have never seen scars caused by having parts of a man's body such as his neck, wrists, or feet chained for long periods of time, then try to imagine them. No hair grows on those scars, and the scars look milky white and are as hard as leather.

This is the kind of back Paul of Tarsus must have had after being beaten by Jewish whips (thirty-nine lashes) five times. Beyond that, three beatings by Roman birch rods, which would be far more horrific than any Jewish beating with a whip. Enduring constant pain from even the slightest movement, from stretching, and the chance that someone not knowing what his back looked like might suddenly bump up against him. Such was the body of Paul of Tarsus, and such were the scars of Prem Pradhan.

The greatest honor of my life, other than that of being married to Helen, is the high privilege of having worked with Prem Pradhan. We sat together on numerous occasions in my home and in conferences.

One day I had the privilege of interviewing Prem.

I asked him the name and the place of each of his five imprisonments. He immediately recalled the names of the prisons, then gave me a description of them and their exact locations. He could even explain what had happened to him during the four years he lived in each of the four prisons, which totals sixteen years in prison. (There was a fifth imprisonment, but he stayed only one day. However, that was probably the most harrowing day of all.)

Prem always started his testimony by saying, "I come from a tiny little country just north of India called Nepal."

Nepal has some very interesting laws. If you changed religions to something other than the one into which you were born, you went to prison for one year. If you preached the message of this new religion, you would go to prison for four years. Prem has a historic position no other man in the world has ever had or ever will have. Prem was the first person ever to become a Christian in Nepal and also, at the same time, the first apostle to Nepal. Further, the next hundred, two hundred, or three hundred converts were all led to Christ by one man, Prem Pradhan. They were won to the Lord during and after his first four-year term in prison. (He usually converted all the prisoners while he was imprisoned with them.)

The first Christian church planted in Nepal was started by Prem. That church was made up primarily of people Prem had led to the Lord and baptized while they were in prison.

Here's how Prem was converted. He was a captain in the Nepalese army and receiving special training in India when he heard some people preaching the gospel on the streets. Prem rushed over to them and asked a question that had plagued him throughout his life. "What can I do to keep from going to hell?" He had a great fear of hell.

They told him about Jesus Christ, and on that same day he received Christ and was baptized.

The Christians who led Prem to the Lord told him to read the entire Bible every six weeks and to read the New Testament once every week. Prem said, "I do this for twenty years, but I not learn Bible; I learn Jesus. Jesus more important than Bible."

Whenever Prem preached to his people in Nepal, he always added: "Now, you not come to Christ unless you willing to be baptized and go to prison for one year."

Amazingly, they responded, were baptized, and went to prison for one year.

One of the first things Prem told me that caught my attention was this: "I come to America; I see riches. Everybody wish to listen to me. I go home, my people say, 'Show us pictures.' I do not take pictures. My people do not understand buildings, pulpit, pews, preachers standing up talking and talking, but no one ever doing anything practical. When I meet people who meet in homes in America, they sing songs; they share. I take many pictures. My people can understand this."

Prem observed this while he was speaking at a national gathering of Christians who meet in homes.

While visiting in the United States, Prem delivered a long series of messages on suffering. I requested the messages be transcribed and put into print. When the transcription was finished and handed to me, I had expected there to be several hundred pages of his messages. Instead, there were only fifty. I asked, "Where is the rest?"

I was told, "Prem repeated the same thing in five messages: 'If you are a Christian, you must suffer.'"

Have you ever heard the term *a Christian presence*? The term is used when a nation does not allow the preaching of the gospel. This goes as far as not allowing anyone to even speak the words Jesus Christ. Nepal does not allow the preaching of the gospel; nonetheless, Christian missionaries have established a "Christian presence" in Nepal. That means Christian missionaries have built hospitals, schools, orphanages, and outpatient clinics. All of these are run by Christians, but the gospel of Jesus Christ is never mentioned.

Then, suddenly, Prem appeared. Here was a native of Nepal who was baptized and had gone to prison for changing his religion. Every denomination which had established "a Christian presence" in Nepal asked Prem to join them and become a worker under the umbrella of that denomination. Prem declined.

He told them, "I am just a simple Christian. I have nothing in front of my name or after my name. Keep your money. I no want your money. I no want to come to America. I no want to be rich. I no want to be famous. I want to preach the gospel to my people. I want my people to go to prison for one year after they are baptized. I must also go to prison. I stay in prison. I make prison Christian."

This extraordinary decision gave insight into Prem's view of what a Christian—and a Christian worker—ought to be.

Prem was true to his word. Whenever he preached the gospel, he told those who listened at the beginning, at the middle, and at the end of his speaking: "Do not become a Christian unless you willing to go to prison for one year."

I often heard him say, "In America all Christians should go to prison for one year. America has too many Christians. You would not have large numbers of Christians if every Christian had to go to Nepal prison for one year."

At the time I met Prem, he had been in prison longer than he had been out of prison during his Christian life.

Prem went to prison five times. The first time he went to prison, he was a nuisance. The second and third times he went to prison, they realized that Nepal had a serious problem, so they tried to kill him. After the fourth time he was in prison, he had become a legend in

Nepal, even to the point that now the government was interested in protecting him.

The first time Prem was imprisoned was one of the worst. That prison was the most infamous prison in Nepal and the most inhumane. Nonetheless, four years later he was released from prison and every inmate in that prison was a baptized Christian. After Prem was released, he continued preaching the gospel and raised up several churches. Among the members were ones who had been saved during his first imprisonment.

While Prem was in prison for the second time, the missionaries bought Prem's converts. I mean by that, they paid each of them $75 a year just for attending the missionaries' compound. Anyone who had been trained by Prem and was a worker was paid the astronomical sum of $275 a year. (The average income in Nepal was $75 a year per family.) When Prem got out of prison the second time, there was not a single Christian there to greet him, nor anyone to gather with him. Every soul had been purchased by foreign money.

It was in the second prison that the government authorities decided to make sure that this troublesome man would die. The people in Nepal are not used to murder; therefore, the authorities came up with an idea for murder by other means. Prem was placed in a small room that contained some corpses of those who had died in prison. In this small room containing dead bodies, he was chained on both his hands and feet. He could not even consider escaping. His only escape from that room would be by dying of cholera. But Prem did not catch cholera.

Eventually, the corpses had to be removed. Their conclusion was, if we cannot kill him by exposing him to dead, rotting bodies, we will freeze him to death. So, Prem was staked out in the snow to die of exposure in the cruel, harsh weather of the Himalaya Mountains. I remember so clearly what he said: "I praised God for being staked in the snow; it killed all the lice on me, praise God."

By now, the guards and those who were in the prison were getting a little spooked by this man who apparently could not be killed nor stopped from preaching about Christ. He was brought back into the prison. Every day Prem preached the gospel to those in jail, and little by little, one by one, those prisoners received Christ as their Savior and were baptized in the prison.

What of Prem's third imprisonment? Prem was put into the prison that was the farthest north in Nepal. The people in that prison were among the worst of the criminal element in that country. During his imprisonment, there was an attempt at an escape. In fact, it succeeded. Prem was in his cell when the leader of the rebellion killed all the guards. He came to Prem and said, "You must leave."

Prem said, "I will not be part of what you do."

The leader then said, "I will kill you."

Prem answered, "Then kill me. I no leave."

The man raised a rifle and aimed it straight at Prem's head and pulled the trigger. The gun did not fire. The man checked the rifle and once more aimed the rifle straight at Prem's head while Prem looked his would-be killer straight in the eye. The second time the rifle would not fire. The man checked his rifle again and aimed it at Prem. This time Prem stood up and said, "You no pull trigger! Twice God has saved you from killing me. You pull that trigger another time, you go straight to hell and you stay in hell and you burn forever and ever."

For a moment, the man did not move. He looked at the rifle, then looked at Prem. He ran from the cell and the prison. When authorities from nearby towns were alerted to the prison break, there were no officers, no guards, as they had all been murdered. All the remaining prisoners, under fear of being shot by the escapees, had also left the prison. The only person remaining was Prem Pradhan, and he was very much alive. The insurrectionists were later captured and sentenced to death. It was after that, Prem became a legend.

During Prem's fourth imprisonment he was treated like a celebrity. But he was left alone. He could do whatever he wished, including preach the gospel.

<hr />

When Prem was visiting in the United States, men heard of his healing powers and one instance of his raising the dead. Some of them came to him to inquire about the secret to his power. Prem knew the reason they wanted power was so they could become famous.

Prem answered these men, and he spoke in great anger: "If you want power with God, you must suffer. If you want power with God, come with me to Nepal: you preach gospel, you go to prison four years. God will break you, but He still not give you power. If God give you power the way your heart is today, He give you power to destroy you. He not give you power to heal; He give you power so He can destroy you. God give power to most men to destroy those men.

"You go back to Nepal with me a second time, you go to prison, you come out four more years, you still unbroken, God not give you power. You go to prison third time, God pay attention to you. He make you suffer even more than first time and second time. Maybe He take your life, maybe He let you live. God break you a little, then He break you again and again. No more you will want power. You want God to go away and leave you alone, that is all you will want. But, He keep on breaking you and breaking you: you have no interest in power any more.

"Then God give you a little power. If you keep on hating the power and you keep on pouring out life on God's people, if Christ become all you want, then maybe God give you a little of His power, but your heart will be for the people, not for you. Your heart will be for Jesus, not for you. Then He break you again and again until the day you die. You sure you want power?"

The men who heard Prem's words walked away, not wanting anything to do with the kind of power of which Prem had spoken.

While speaking at one of the gatherings made up of Christians who meet in homes, Prem observed: "I like the way you meet. You are simple. People talk. Everybody talk. Everybody praise God. Nobody call me doctor."

———— ∼∼∼ ————

Once Prem invited me to Nepal: "You come to Nepal. Nobody arrest you because you born Christian. You born in Christian nation." Then he added, "We will hold a conference. We hold meetings in riverbed. We eat millet." That is all the description he gave. We set the time and the date.

It was there on the living room floor of my home that Prem told me the following story.

"Every time I come out of prison, no churches. Four times I come out of prison, four times Western money had bought all my people. All my people follow missionaries. Now there are churches in Nepal that are Westernized."

Then he told me a story about one particular church. The story was heartbreaking. The leaders of one particular denomination came, and all the Christians of Prem's church were asked to gather for a photograph. A big banner in English was placed over the group. None of them could read English. None of them knew what was happening, but the banner in English said: "This is the work of your denomination. This church belongs to ———." The sign named the denomination.

The photograph was taken back to America and was printed and sent to all the churches of that denomination. In that letter, they asked for money to be sent to this group of Christians in Nepal: "Send money so we can help our sister church in Nepal." The money came pouring in from America. Then the missionaries of that denomination used that money to buy the Christians who were in Prem's church.

This story continued: "Many times American missionaries come and take pictures of me and show pictures of the churches I raised up in prison. They send pictures back to America. They asked, 'Send money to help Prem Pradhan raise up churches in Nepal.' Money comes in—lots of money. The money is used not to help me, but to buy the people I preached the gospel to in prison. These missionaries pay them to be Christians, and my people become Westernized. Soon they sit in pews, they sing Western songs put to Nepalese words, a preacher preaches, people sing again, and everybody go home."

At the end of this story, I asked Prem a question. I was asking this question of a man who had been beaten, a man who had suffered unbelievably in and out of prisons. All of this was inflicted by the government of Nepal.

Here was the question: "Prem, who has caused you the greatest suffering . . . your government which has imprisoned you, beaten you, and tried to kill you, or the Western missionaries?"

I can still hear his answer as he moved his hands in the tradition of people from Nepal emphasizing their words by the movements of their fingers: "Oh, no comparison. I suffer far, far more at hands of Christians than ever I suffer from government in Nepal."

Prem succeeded in raising up a group of Nepalese workers who met together twice a year. There was great hope at this time for the future work in Nepal. "Then I was taken again to prison. When I got out, I called for a meeting of my workers. One of the missionaries told me, 'You are not allowed to come to this meeting.'"

"Why?" I asked. "I led these men to Jesus. I trained them. We worked together for gospel. Why I not come to meeting?"

The missionary replied, "You are no longer welcome among your workers. They are now all pastors of churches and receive their income as gifts from the West."

Prem had been asked: "The next time you go to prison and you come out to find your work has been taken over by others, will you not consider quitting?"

Prem answered the question in fury. "I will never quit! As long as I live, I will go on preaching the gospel and raising up churches in Nepal. When I die, then I quit!"

What of Prem's fifth and last imprisonment? This time some leaders in the Nepal government put him in an insane asylum. They decided to place him in a cell with a cannibal who killed people in order to drink their blood. He was a man of massive strength. Prem was pushed into the cell. He backed against the wall and waited. Whether or not he realized it, he had actually backed up against the door. As the madman approached Prem, the door opened. The man who opened the door was no less than the brother of the king of Nepal.

While Prem had been out of prison, the brother of the king of Nepal had invited Prem to come to him. They had had several meetings, and Prem had shared the gospel with him. Whether or not the man had become a Christian, I do not know. But this we do know: his sympathies had shifted to Prem and his people. Prem was taken out of the cell and out of the prison. The king's brother made it clear to the authorities through-out Nepal that Prem Pradhan was never to be arrested again for preaching the gospel and was to be treated as one of the leading citizens of the country.

On the day word reached me that Prem had died, the spontaneous words coming out of my mouth were: "Prem, no! Don't do that! Don't die!"

How did Prem die? Prem was doing what Prem did throughout his life. He was on a narrow trail going up into an almost unknown village, high in the Himalayas, where he planned to preach the gospel. One of the main arteries in his body ruptured and he died instantly. He was buried along the wayside.

In my judgment, Prem belongs to a pantheon of less than a half-dozen men who lived wholly for Jesus Christ under the most dire circumstances.

One of the greatest honors of my life has been that Prem was my closest and dearest friend. Prem showed all of us what a man called of God is to be.

# CHAPTER 26

# THE ICE TOWER

It was 1:00 a.m. I recognized the voice on the other end of the phone as one of the owners of the oil company for which I worked. He called me by my nickname. All oil-field roughnecks have a nickname, and I doubt any of us actually know the real names of one another.

"Rockbit, can you get to the Cold Springs location within twenty minutes?"

"No," I responded, "but I think I can make it in twenty-five."

"There is a norther coming in from Canada. It is

one of the coldest on record. Southeast Texas has been receiving a torrent of rain for weeks. When that norther hits, it is going to freeze that end of Texas. We need every roughneck possible to go to Cold Springs to keep the well there operating. If we shut down for three or four days, we will lose the well."

"Where is Blackie?"

"He is probably at the location not too far from Shepherd, but our mobile phone is on the blink. We will keep trying to call him. If Blackie doesn't get there, we will surely lose the well."

I replied, "Blackie has never lost a well in his life."

"We know that, but if that rig freezes, we will lose the well."

We hung up. The first thing I did was throw a sheet on the floor in the living room of the tiny house where I lived. I began throwing canned goods onto the sheet, along with anything else I could think of which would not spill. I gathered up the four corners, tied them in a knot, and threw it in the back seat of my car.

I also reached into the trunk to pull out four tire chains. The tire chains were made to be wrapped around the tires like a glove made out of steel. They would keep me from getting stuck if the roads froze over. I then shot over to the only gas station open that late at night, purchased six five-gallon cans of gasoline, and placed them in the trunk of my car.

When I left my home in Cleveland, Texas, it was raining and the wind was blowing hard. About five miles out, the norther hit and began freezing everything in sight. I could not have stayed on the road without those steel tire chains. Eventually, my windshield began to ice over. Inside my car was a searchlight, as was true of many cars owned by oil-field workers. Very shortly, the snow was so thick that the bright searchlight no longer showed me a road.

I stuck my head out the window and continued on, stopping frequently to remove the ice from my face. I finally had to open the door and managed to keep my foot on the gas pedal at the same time.

I eventually arrived in Cold Springs, turned onto a country road, and faced what would be nearly impossible— driving a completely iced-over wood-plank road for more than a mile, deep into the heart of the woods. We had built that plank road out of boards four inches thick and twelve feet long. This road was now solid ice.

I eased up onto the plank road and very cautiously drove into the foreboding woods. I managed to get to the end of the plank road, and my searchlight revealed two things. One was a seven-story-high derrick, which was now a tower of ice. The second was something that in oil-field lingo is called "the doghouse." It was a small mobile home with few conveniences. At that moment, it looked like we were going to be marooned for at least a week.

I looked back at the tower of ice. If the mud and cement did not circulate by the end of three days, we would lose the well. In my opinion, under no conditions known to man or angels was anyone going to save that well.

I walked into the doghouse. I still remember the names of the men who were there. I was grateful to know that I was marooned with seven of the best, toughest, bravest roughnecks in Texas. Their names were Grunt, Mopey, Runt, Stump, Brother, and Little Brother. Then there was Tarz, the driller. The only person over him was Blackie, who supervised three different drilling locations. I was the youngest roughneck in the room, age seventeen, but I had been a roughneck since I was fourteen.

"Has anyone been able to reach Blackie?"

"Yeah, just a minute ago."

Now, it's worth noting that Blackie was an oil-field legend. He never told a story about himself, but every man who ever worked with him had stories to tell.

Blackie had once hired a young man named Red who knew nothing about oil wells. Red later became the most famous man in the oil-field business, making his living putting out oil-field fires. His charge was one million dollars per fire. I might add, he deserved it. When Red was putting out a fire, if that fire should reignite, Red himself would become an inferno.

Red would never admit this, but Blackie was the person who not only hired Red into the oil-field business as a roughneck, but also taught him how to put out a fire. To his credit, Red saw much more financial potential in putting out fires than Blackie did and as a result became one of the wealthiest men in Texas.

Blackie also hired another man who became a legend in the oil-field business. His name was Glenn McCarthy. Glenn was known for being a millionaire one year and poverty stricken the next. He had just recently built a hotel in Houston called the Shamrock.

The most uncanny thing about Blackie was his ability to tell whether or not there was oil five thousand feet below the surface of the earth. One time Haliburton came out to take a core sample. There, men who had doctorate degrees in petroleum engineering would use chemicals to examine the core. Blackie would have none of these fancy methods of finding out if there was oil down there. He simply took the core sample, bit into it, and chewed on it. It did not matter what the petroleum engineers had decided; when Blackie gave his opinion, it was Blackie's opinion that prevailed.

Blackie was an unlikely genius. He grew up in an illiterate French Cajun family in the poorest county in America. On the day he married, he could neither read nor write his name, but he had already shown his genius in solving the myriad problems that arose in drilling for oil. Perhaps the thing for which he was best known among the men who worked for him was his superhuman strength.

Back to the doghouse, we were all waiting for Blackie to arrive, and we saw the headlights of a car working its way down that icy wood-plank road. Almost simultaneously we all said, "It's Blackie!"

Blackie came in the doghouse. It was Tarz who stated the obvious: "Blackie, we're going to lose this well."

Blackie didn't say a word. He walked out and took a long look at that tower. The ground outside the doghouse was covered in ice three or four inches thick. The stairs leading up to the floor of the derrick, which was twelve feet above the ground, were covered with ice. There was no metal showing anywhere. On one side of the rig we had built a steel ladder, which was exactly eight inches wide and seven stories high. The distance between each rung of the ladder was twelve inches.

Blackie managed to get over to our toolshed. He came out with a holster, put a wrench in it, wrapped it around his waist, and began walking toward that seven-story tower of ice.

"Blackie is going to try to save that well," someone yelled.

"It can't be done," someone else said.

"It will cost him his life!"

All of us instinctively ran for our cars and turned our search lights on Blackie. It was 2:30 a.m. I had full assurance that I was going to watch Blackie die that night, plummeting seven stories to the ground.

Blackie began to beat away the ice from the stairs leading up to the floor. Over and over again he slipped, but there was always one hand holding onto the side railing. He then beat off a path of ice leading to a place where he could climb the ladder, covered in three inches of ice.

Over and over again Blackie beat ice off one side of that ladder, and then the other, until the ladder was cleared for about a foot. Then we watched him do what few men on earth could do. With one fist wrapped around solid ice and often with both legs dangling, Blackie lifted his entire body with the strength of one arm until his waist was at the same height as his fist.

Someone whispered, "I know that man is tough, but I've never seen anything like that in my life."

Someone else added, "No, and neither has anyone else!"

That was Blackie's long journey upward, beating ice off each rung of the ladder, holstering the wrench, pulling himself up to the next rung, and then beating the stubborn, almost immovable ice off the next rung.

We watched this for hours. Finally, Blackie arrived at the fence around the crown of the derrick. After beating the ice off about two feet of the fence, Blackie managed to get to the giant spool of cable at the very top of the derrick. If he slipped, it would be an eighty-foot drop to the ground.

Finally, with those two plier-like hands, Blackie lifted himself up, mounted the huge spool of cable, and began beating away the ice that had imprisoned it.

One of the things that was so curious about Blackie was that he never bragged; he never showed off. But he was keenly aware of who he was and what he was doing. He had a gold tooth, and on rare occasions he would grin so big that you could see that gold tooth. He would then chuckle just a little and smile. This was Blackie's way of saying, "I did it!"

We all stood there dumbfounded. What happened next was truly unexpected. Blackie, a man who was only five feet, six inches tall, stood to his full height, doubled up his fists, and raised his arms in the gesture of a prize fighter who had just won a boxing match. When Blackie did that, with all those beams of search lights flooding upward, all of us exclaimed at the same time . . .

"King Kong!"

We all began to cheer. We quickly went to our cars and began honking our horns and flashing those search-lights all over the derrick, the crown, and Blackie.

The next thing Blackie did was even more dangerous. To this day, I still do not know how he did it. Underneath that spool there dangled one strand of cable that led down about thirty feet to the giant block and tackle. We watched in horror as Blackie slid down that thirty-foot ice-covered cable which reached down to the block and tackle. He stood there on the block and tackle for a moment, totally isolated.

After Blackie had beaten the ice off the derrick's crown, it was then possible in the hands of a master driller, to break loose the ice on the giant spool of cable that rested on the floor. We all struck out of the dog-house and slid, climbed, and fell until we got up to the floor of the rig. With whatever tool we had, we began beating on the main cable, setting it free. That enabled us to start the diesel engines.

Now, gradually, Tarz was able to bring the block and tackle down to the floor. He began moving no more than an inch of cable upward, then an inch downward. Little flakes of ice all the way from the crown to where

Blackie was marooned began to fall. Tarz did this again and again. It must have been thirty minutes, but little by little the ice was coming off the spool of cable and the remainder of the ice on the crown of that derrick. Little by little, by moving the block and tackle upward and downward, Tarz had freed the entire cable system of all ice. In the meantime, Blackie held onto that ice covered cable, being certain that Tarz could somehow break the lock the ice had on everything inside the heart of that derrick.

The block weighed more than a school bus and was almost as big.

Blackie did not move off of it. That monstrous block and tackle slowly began to lie down on the derrick's floor. It was almost completely down when Blackie jumped clear of it and landed on the no longer ice-covered floor.

A few minutes later, the men were back at their cars, honking their horns and flashing what looked like a blazing inferno of light coming from that tower.

The next day, and for the next several weeks, everyone on that side of Texas who knew anything about the oil-field world, was telling the story of Blackie and how he saved a frozen well. Before that night was over, we had spudded in and were lifting the pipe out of the ground and forcing it back into the earth to make sure neither the mud nor the cement congealed.

Now go back with me to the moment when Blackie stepped off the derrick. He was covered with ice. I ran as fast as I could to my car while Blackie staggered down the stairs. I turned my heater all the way up and began throwing all the quilts I had brought into the back seat. Blackie came over to my car, opened the door, and sat down. I was horrified at what I saw. He was shaking all over. Ice was caked on his entire body . . . on his clothes and under his clothes. He was perspiring like nothing I had ever seen, and steam was coming off his body.

A few minutes after Blackie got into my car, he asked, "Boy, you warm?" I responded, "Yes sir, I am warm." Blackie grinned, his gold tooth showing.

Blackie knew that in these four hours he had done something no other man on earth could possibly have done. Who was this quiet Louisiana Cajun . . . so loved, so respected, and even revered?

Blackie grew up in poverty and ignorance that few could hardly imagine. At fifteen years of age, Blackie walked into a brush arbor meeting near Winnfield, Louisiana, barefooted and wearing a denim shirt and trousers and a rope for a belt. Those were the only clothes he owned. He could neither read, nor write, nor spell his name. At the end of the meeting, Blackie went forward, fell on his knees, and received Christ as his Savior.

In Texas, twenty years after his conversion, he was married and had two sons. Blackie saw his younger son come down with diphtheria, followed by rheumatic fever, then scarlet fever. Finally, he developed pneumonia. It was no surprise when one day the doctor announced to Blackie and his wife, "Your son will not live through the night." With that, Blackie gathered up all the medicine in the house and flushed it.

The home became a death vigil. The boy was burning with fever. The doctor came to the home twice every day. The three-year-old boy struggled with every breath, as both lungs filled with fluid.

Finally, shaking with great sobs, Blackie fell to his knees and began to bargain with the Lord. "Let him live and we will make no claims on his life. He is Yours alone to do whatever You want done." Moments later, the fever broke. Against all odds, the boy lived.

Need I tell you? I was that three-year-old boy. I am that younger son.

Now, with all the pride and all the honor that a child can possibly have for his parents, I tell you that Blackie Edwards is *my* father.

# ACKNOWLEDGMENTS

To Di Mercer and Robyn Frank, who so brilliantly and faithfully typed this manuscript, along with my precious wife, Helen, who is a master of English grammar and who has made every day of my life enchanted.

To Joel Kneedler, friend and publisher, and the brilliant Joey Paul, who served as editor of *Stories I Love to Tell*, along with Janene MacIvor.

# ABOUT THE AUTHOR

Gene Edwards is one of America's most-beloved Christian authors. He has published more than twenty-five bestselling books. His signature work, *The Divine Romance*, has been called a masterpiece of Christian literature. He has written biblical fiction covering nearly the entire Bible, with titles that include: *The Beginning*, *The Escape*, *The Birth*, *The Divine Romance*, *The Triumph*, *Revolution*, *The Silas Diary*, *The Titus Diary*, *The Timothy Diary*, *The Priscilla Diary*, *The Gaius Diary*, and *The Return*.

Gene grew up in the East Texas oil fields and entered college at the age of fifteen. He graduated from East Texas State University at eighteen with a bachelor's degree in English history and received his MDiv from Southwestern Baptist Theological Seminary. Gene is part of the house church movement, and he travels extensively to aid Christians as they begin meeting in homes rather than in church buildings. He also conducts conferences on living the deeper Christian life.

Gene and his wife, Helen, reside in Jacksonville, Florida, and have two grown children.

A GIFT FOR:

----------------------------------------------------------------

FROM:

----------------------------------------------------------------

# THE RED SUIT DIARIES

------ **VOLUME TWO** ------

# the *red suit* diaries

------ VOLUME TWO ------

*santa shares*
more hopes, dreams,
and childlike faith

BY ED BUTCHART

Published by Hallmark Books,
a division of Hallmark Cards, Inc.,
Kansas City, MO 64141
Visit us on the Web at www.Hallmark.com.

Editorial Director: Todd Hafer
Art Director: Kevin Swanson
Designer: Michelle Nicole Nicolier
Production Artist: Dan Horton

ISBN: 978-1-59530-179-6
BOK6069
Printed and bound in China

To the god who loves me and continues
to bless me far beyond my deserving

# the *diaries*

------------ **VOLUME TWO** ------------

Dear Diary,

There have been a lot of things that have influenced my life as Santa. But none has had a more profound and personal impact than the death of my Annie, my wonderful Mrs. Claus. It was the winter of 2004. She had been sick for a long time and had been in the ICU four times over the years. A couple of those times, her doctors told me there was nothing more they could do for her. But hard praying—and her amazingly strong will to live—made her health improve and allowed her to come home again.

This time, however, was different. This time she told me she just couldn't pull off another miraculous recovery. She was just too tired and weak to do it again. I begged her not to leave me. I told her I could not go on without her, and particularly could not go on being Santa. But she told me that I had to keep going. There were too many kids who believed in me, she said, and our love for Jesus demanded that I keep sharing that love with kids and adults. She told me not to mourn. She knew where she was going, and whom she would be with, and she wanted me to go on and be happy again. She slipped into a coma two days later, and died on the one of most important days in our lives: Christmas.

The reaction of my family and friends was amazing. A good friend (and a fellow Santa), in High Point, North Carolina, sent me an e-mail that said, "Boy, don't you know Annie had a glorious Christmas Day." My oldest son, Paul, responded, "That's great, Dad. Now you have something else to celebrate on Christmas: Annie's going home to heaven."

And that was so true. Annie was taken into the arms of Jesus, on the very day that we celebrate His birth. She was freed from all her pain, all the medications, and given a perfect new body and home in heaven on the day she and I had commemorated so many times in our red suits. We had always prayed that our portrayals would demonstrate and emulate God's love for His people. I know her love did just that.

# finding *peace*

## AIRBRAKE MCGUIRTY

For several summers I've been playing a character in a replica 1870s town—called Crossroads Village—at Stone Mountain Park. My character was Airbrake McGuirty, a railroad engineer, complete with requisite blue-and-white-striped overalls and hat. I was still grieving the loss of my Annie, and going to Stone Mountain Park and becoming someone else for a few hours a day was good therapy. It helped me to see that my life still had purpose.

Here's how Airbrake was born. In 2000, the management company at Stone Mountain Park opened the first element of Crossroads Village: a hamburger restaurant, with a grand opening scheduled for Memorial Day weekend. The theme of the restaurant was a diner for railroad crews, and the creators wanted a character to act as a host and entertainer—to greet customers and make them feel at home. They handed me a pair of striped overalls, a matching hat, and a work shirt and asked if I could create a character. I added a bandana, work gloves, and a pump oilcan with a long spout—the kind railroad men used to keep the steam locomotives running smoothly.

Nobody told me exactly what I should do other than "just entertain folks." When the ribbon was cut and the first customers arrived, I stood by the door and greeted them, helped them decipher the menu and place their orders. I tried to keep it light, bantering back and forth in my Airbrake persona. But it was only a few moments before my beard caught some visitors' attention. There was no way I could escape the Santa association. No matter how much I protested, I couldn't avoid it. So I decided to make that part of the fun.

I was carrying the oilcan around, but couldn't figure out how to work it into my routine. When I spied the ketchup pump, inspiration hit me. I went into the kitchen, opened the oilcan, and poured it full of ketchup. I pumped it into the sink a few times to make sure it worked, then went back into the dining room.

I went up to a kid just about ready to bite into his hamburger and asked, "How are the French fries?" Before he could reply, I said, "You need a little motor oil on them, don't you think?" Just as I started to pump, his Mom yelped. When she saw it was just ketchup, she laughed. I knew I had found my gimmick. It was an easy way to divert attention away from my beard.

Unfortunately, I didn't wash out the can every night, and the acid in the tomatoes began to work on the metal parts of the pump. The ketchup tasted terrible! So I put the gimmick aside for a few days. Then I found a home-made toy a friend had given me. He called it a "hooey stick." It was two pieces of wood of two different lengths. One was about a foot long and had a series of notches cut into its edges, with a small rectangular propeller attached at one end by a nail. The other piece of wood was about four inches long. The trick was to rub the small one along the notches on the big one and make the propeller turn. By skillful manipulation of the small stick, you could change the direction in which the propeller turned.

Kids and adults were amazed! They could not figure out how the contraption worked. To enhance the mystery, I would say the "secret word" just before the propeller reversed direction. The secret word was "hooey." And when someone asked me how it worked, I'd reply, "It's just a bunch of hooey!" That silly trick has worked for more than four years now, and it has brought a lot of fun into people's lives, including my own. I had a friend of mine produce 500 hooey sticks. I packaged them in kits and sold them in Crossroads' gift shops. Thanks to the generous management at the park, all the proceeds went to my ministry, Friends of Disabled Adults and Children. And anyone who bought one of the kits was entitled to one free hooey lesson from me.

## THE ADVENTURES
## OF AIRBRAKE

Being Airbrake was and is wonderful therapy for me. It gives me a chance to have in-depth visits with a lot of folks. I walk along the queues where the people are waiting to board the trains, talking to folks about where they're from and how they like the park. Many people ask if I am Santa Claus. Most of the time I feign surprise that anyone would even make that connection. Then I slyly add, "Come back at Christmas and find out."

I do have a few ploys for avoiding direct questions about Santa, and most of the time it works. I tell people, "I'm not Santa; I'm the Easter Bunny!" Nobody believes that, of course, and I usually wind up whispering, "Shhh, don't tell anybody. I am in disguise." That will usually work until they board the train and are pulling out of the station. Then there is a chorus of, "Bye, Santa Claus!" from all the kids—and lots of the adults.

My primary job as Airbrake is to make the wait for the

train seem shorter by entertaining with my hooey stick and engaging people in conversation. We host many international visitors, and it is always a treat to try to communicate with them. I do okay with Spanish, German, and American Sign Language. I've found that many Europeans speak German, so we can often find a connection there. But mostly I just blunder on and probably make a big fool of myself. But, what the heck? I do that in English, too.

Some fun happens when a kid or parent recognizes me because they've seen me as Stone Mountain's Santa earlier on. And believe me, it's hard to deny my Santa identity to anyone who's seen me in my red suit.

Sometimes, it can work in reverse. Once, I was in my full Santa gear, eating at a wonderful seafood restaurant in High Point, North Carolina. A lady came up to my table and said, "Hello, Santa. The last time I saw you, you were wearing a blue-and-white-striped outfit."

I was stunned. "My goodness! How in the world did you recognize me?"

"By the twinkle in your eye!" she said.

What a wonderful compliment that was.

Many of the people we see at the park are with tour groups, and that adds a new dimension to our encounters. On one occasion, there was a large crowd of tour folks waiting for the train, and I asked if there were any rich widows in the group. To my surprise, four women raised their hands. I picked out a pretty lady in the middle and said, "Tell me about it."

She answered, "Well, I own my own home outright, and I have lots of money in the bank. I also have a brand-new Cadillac and a big monthly income."

I said, "Wow! Would you marry me?"

She laughed real loud and said, "Are you kidding me? Marry you and mess all that up? Forget it!" The crowd roared and applauded. I couldn't help but laugh myself.

Every afternoon at 5:30, all of the actors in the park gather for the Sundown Social event at the gazebo in front of the train station. There is a lot of singing and dancing—and a huge amount of fun. It always ends with the Tennessee Waltz, and the audience is invited to join in.

The characters choose partners from the audience while everyone else sways to the music. It's a wonderful time. And it would be even better if I knew how to dance. The kids are often dancing right up front, watching me intently to see what I'm going to do. I asked a staff member to dance one time, and we did okay, but I could feel the eyes of the audience on my beard and barely kept myself from taking a nosedive.

When the social is over, all the characters are released for the day, except for me. I go back to the train and continue playing with the passengers. It might seem like drudgery, but it's not. Occasionally, I get to ride the train. I latch onto a kid or friendly adult and accompany them on the five-mile trip. I have a chance to interact with them—and they have a chance to ask me all the important questions of life, like, "Are you Santa Claus?" "Where are your reindeer?" "Why are you here?" "Am I on the good-kid list?"

I wear a name tag with "Airbrake" on it, and even though I keep pointing to it and asserting, "I'm not Santa," for some reason, folks just don't believe me!

I also have the freedom to walk through Crossroads and see people in other parts of the village. I usually just walk up to folks and ask how they are doing, where they are from, and how they like our little park. I try to think of myself as the host of the village and to treat people like they are guests in my home. I always ask if they have any questions about the park or if they need directions or suggestions to get the most out of their visits. I let them know that the park has 3,200 acres, and there are many places scattered throughout that you don't want to miss. It is definitely worth visiting, and it takes at least a couple of days to see it all. So y'all come see us, now, you hear?

Lots of folks have asked me about the Santa encounters I described in the first volume of *The Red Suit Diaries.* So I'm thinking that you might want to know what has happened to some of the people I wrote about.

I get the most questions about the little boy who told me that all he wanted for Christmas was for his dad to quit beating him. He showed me marks and scars on his hands, neck, and ears. It was clear that he was being abused. I told him God loved him and I loved him, and that we wanted the abuse to stop. I encouraged him to tell his favorite teacher what was going on. He promised he would, but I never heard another word about him. I think of him often and wonder what is happening in his life. I hope I'll see him someday.

Another one I hear a lot of questions about is the "grown-up little girl," Rachel. Her worst handicap was not her mental disability but her family's attitude about it. I only saw her once, but I'll never forget the adoring look on her thirty-year-old face as she told me what she wanted for Christmas. Her eyes were full of the kind of wonder you usually only see in very young children.

Her mother told me, "You don't have to mess with her. She ain't right, ain't never been right. You can forget about her." I told her mother that God loved her just like He did all His children, and I would show her God's love with my love. The mother walked away mumbling as her precious daughter sat on my lap and gave me her list. My only regret was that I couldn't just hand her the Barbie doll and other things she asked for, since I didn't think I could trust her family to get them for her.

Though I'm sad I never saw that boy or woman again, I'm grateful to have had the opportunity to meet and get to know some other wonderful kids. You may remember Cody Cooper. Cody, a near-drowning survivor, was two years old when we met. His mother told me that she didn't know how long Cody would be with them, but that she was going to love him every minute that he lived. And live he did—for 16 more years. His body finally could not sustain life, and he died peacefully in February of 2005.

I had promised his mother years before that I would help with his funeral when the time came and, in spite of my own grief at the time, I did. It was a glorious celebration of a life that had touched so many people. And it was the dedication of Cody's parents, Judy and Henry, that helped make Cody's life all it could be. They had taken him to Alaska and many places out West. He saw a pod of Orcas in the wild—something most kids (and most adults!) will never experience. Although Cody never spoke and never had any voluntary movements, he was able to reach others, including me, with a message of love and acceptance of all people.

I also stayed close with Lindsay Brown's family. A year before we met, the Santa at the mall would not touch Lindsay and told her mother to move her out of the way. The next year, I called them down off the balcony and took Lindsay out of her wheelchair and into my arms. It didn't matter to me that she had a breathing tube in her nose and feeding tube in her stomach. Lindsay's mother, Jane, informed me that when her daughter was born, doctors had told her that she would not live for a year. She was five when I met her. Like Cody's mother, Judy, Jane told me she was going to love her child as best she could for as long as she lived. And she would do just that for 16 whole years.

Lindsay and Cody never met. But I met them within two weeks of one another. And years later, they died within two weeks of one another. I was talking to Jane on the phone at the moment Lindsay died. I was there at the hospice ten minutes later. Like Cody's, her funeral was a celebration of a life filled with love.

When two-and-a-half-year-old Laura Withers climbed on my lap at Macy's in 1992, she was the most delightful two-year-old I had ever encountered. In fact, at sixteen, she's still delightful. Her dad and mom, Craig and Vicki, are near and dear friends.

On the day Annie died, I came home and sent out an e-mail to all our friends. Twenty minutes later, Vicki called and said she was coming over. I told her she was going to do no such thing. It was Christmas Day, and she should spend it with her family. She hung up on me. Fifteen minutes later, the doorbell rang.

I blocked the door with my 270-pound body and told Vicki to go home. She shoved me out of the way and came in the house. Then she grabbed my arms and taught me a valuable lesson. She said, "You are not the only one grieving. I have to grieve, too. So let me do something. Anything. Cleaning, dusting, anything." I told her I had just had the house completely cleaned on Christmas Eve. (That was the only thing Annie had told me she wanted for Christmas.) Then I thought of something. I grabbed a grocery bag out of the pantry and told her she could collect all of Annie's medications and flush them away. I pointed out the places where she could find them and she went to work. Soon, I heard the commode flushing. Then she told me she would take the bottles with her and dispose of them in her trash can at home. She hugged me and left. The message that visit sent—that others were also hurting, sharing my sense of loss—would stay with me for a very long time.

## REVISITING THE
## EARLY YEARS

After the first *Red Suit Diaries* were published, I remembered a cute story that I wished I'd included. It happened when I was just starting to think about becoming Santa. I had bought a cheap suit, and an even cheaper wig and beard set, and I thought I looked very authentic. I was wrong. I can't even stand to look at pictures from that time. Fortunately, I've come a long way since.

Anyway, right after I obtained my first outfit, a friend who was the principal of a small Lutheran School in Decatur, Georgia, asked me to be Santa for a Christmas party. I knew one five-year-old boy who attended that school, but I figured that with my phony beard, wig, and no glasses, there was no way Richard would recognize me.

When I arrived at the school, I went in the appointed door and stepped into a big room. The kids were all gathered on the other side and did not notice that Santa had sneaked in. I took a deep breath and bellowed, "Merry Christmas, everybody!" The reaction: instant screaming and yelling, jumping up and down, and waving of arms.

Above the din I heard a small male voice yell, "Hey, Mr. Butchart!" I couldn't believe it. How could Richard have made the connection so soon? With my cover blown, I wanted to step out that door again and run away. But I had to be Santa.

The teacher invited me to sit in a big rocking chair and pass out the presents to the kids. I couldn't read the tags with my glasses off, so I told her I would need some boys and girls to help me read the tags. Several of them waved their arms and surged forward to help. There, right in the middle, was Richard waving his arm and shouting, "I'll help you, Mr. Butchart! I'll help you, Mr. Butchart!" I decided that I had to take direct action, so I reached for his wrist.

I smiled, pulled him up to me, and put my mouth to his ear. I whispered playfully in his ear, "Richard, if you call me Mister Butchart one more time I'll break your arm!"

He pulled his head back, his eyes wide. "Okay, Santa Claus!" he said.

I know what you're thinking, and you're right. That was not the right thing to say, and if I had to do it over, I would say it differently. I was a rookie then. I had a lot to learn. I still have a lot to learn, and I hope I never quit learning how to do Santa—and how to do life.

One lesson I am still learning is to be ready for the unexpected. You just never can anticipate what a child might say or do. This one little guy looked about as average as they come. He was just standing, staring, and taking me in when I gestured for him to come to me. He stepped up on my stool and swung his way onto my right leg. As soon as he sat down he exclaimed, "Whoa! You're a lot bigger than I expected."

I leaned back a little and responded, "Well, how big were you expecting?"

He raised his hands and held them about a foot apart. "About this big," he said, his eyes like saucers.

That one took me a moment. "Oh," I said. "That's how big I am on television. In real life I'm much bigger."

He paused for a minute, then finally said, "Okay. Well, here's my list." And he launched into a long, highly sophisticated list of wishes, in order of preference.

There have been some constants in all of my Santa Claus encounters. I still hear the same questions again and again, and I still answer them as though it's the first time I've ever heard them. Many times that gives me a chance to give a mini sermon about the significance of Christmas, and I welcome that opportunity. One of my favorite questions has to do with the roots of Santa's role in the Christmas celebration.

A lot of people don't know the legend of Santa Claus, so they have the mistaken opinion that Santa is a pagan figure with no relationship to the birth of Jesus Christ. Many of them have strong feelings about having Santa included in church celebrations. Unfortunately, some Santas don't know that history either and do a poor job of explaining the connection.

The details are a bit obscure, since they go back hundreds of years. But there is no disputing the fact that the legend of Santa is based on a real man. And not just any man, but a bishop of the early church. His parents had died in one of the devastating plagues that swept Europe. This man, whose name was Nicholas, was left with a large inheritance. And though he was just a boy when his parents passed away, he found himself with the responsibility of caring for the church in his hometown of Myra, a small village in what is now Turkey. Nicholas grew into a strong, healthy man, and was very active in his community. He was still quite young when he was elected as the next bishop.

He was aware of many needy families in his small village, and he used his money to make their lives easier. Sometimes a family needed a specific item, and it would miraculously appear overnight. For example, there was a poor family with four daughters and no way to pay a dowry so that the daughters could marry. As the girls matured one by one, the money required to pay the dowry would mysteriously appear. The coins would be found in the elder sisters' shoes or stockings, which were hung by the fireplace to dry.

Acts of generosity spread throughout that parish—and so did theories about where the funds and items had come from. Nicholas always crept through the village very late at night and since he knew everyone, even all the dogs, he was not confronted by a single creature. After his "miracles" had been told and retold, they began to spread beyond the borders of his country. He was finally unmasked, but the legends, now attributed to Bishop Nicholas, continued to spread.

His parishioners began to call him Saint Nicholas. Years later, the church would make that title official by canonizing him. As the stories and legends spread throughout Europe, his name was transliterated. It became Sinter Klaas in the Netherlands and was ultimately brought to the New World by Dutch immigrants. Eventually the name was anglicized to Santa Claus. This is, of course, a very abridged history. The full story of this man is remarkable. Perhaps that's why there are more churches in the world named for Saint Nicholas than for any other saint.

Thomas Nast, the Civil War-era cartoonist, and Clement Moore, the writer of "A Visit from Saint Nicholas" (later known as "The Night Before Christmas") helped refine the modern image of Santa Claus. Then, Haddon Sunbloom, the artist for the Coca-Cola advertisements of the 1930s and 1940s, further developed that image into the Santa Claus we recognize today. It has nothing to do with paganism and nothing to do with the anti-Christ, but many people don't know the real history of Santa Claus. That's why I enjoy being Santa and sharing his true message of love, acceptance, and generosity.

## THE MARSHMALLOW BOY

Even though it's my job as Santa to be the one who gives gifts, numerous gifts have come my way over the years. One specific story comes to mind. About twelve years ago, Pete, my elf, and I were holding forth on the throne at Stone Mountain Park when a young boy showed up with a white bag with two toasted marshmallows in it. He said, "These are for y'all," handed me the bag, and walked away. Pete and I looked around to see if there were parents involved, but didn't spot any likely suspects. We figured the boy had roasted the marshmallows at the bonfire behind the train station and had brought them to share with us. Not to look ungrateful, we gobbled them up while they were still warm.

A week later, he came by again. More marshmallows—and another quick exit. Still no sign of any parents. Another week, and more marshmallows! Pete dubbed our visitor "The Marshmallow Boy," and that would be our name for him for the eight years that he kept his routine. No matter where the park set us up each year, we could count on The Marshmallow Boy to keep bringing us his special treats.

It was several years before I finally spotted a lady who looked like she could be his mom. We were walking outside. The boy had just handed me the bag, and there she was in the background. I asked her if she was his mom. She told me yes. I hugged her and asked their names. She said his name was Lee Hagan, and her name was Ann. I told her about our name for him, and she got a huge kick out of that. She told me that they lived just outside the west gate to Stone Mountain and considered the park to be their front yard. She had always kept Lee in sight when he was bringing us his marshmallow gifts, even though we'd never noticed her.

From then on, I saw both of them when he stopped by. Then, during the summer I became Airbrake, Ann introduced me to her husband, Jim. He was a delightful guy. He had just retired as a DeKalb County EMT and was going to be a park ranger. I saw him on duty from time to time.

Lee was growing up fast. His parents were both slim but not tall, and he soon surpassed them. When he was sixteen he got his driver's license and began to restore an old car. He came by and kept me posted on his progress. Then his interest switched to motorcycles.

The next thing I knew, he showed up at the train in the uniform of a park ranger. What a fine young man he was becoming.

Then came the nicest surprise of all. Pete and I got invitations to attend the Court of Honor when Lee received his Eagle Scout award. We attended together, and it was an evening of great pride as I heard all the ways our Marshmallow Boy had grown into a terrific young man and wonderful citizen. I knew his parents must be enormously proud—because I felt a measure of vicarious pride myself.

## SECOND - GENERATION
## ENCOUNTERS

The season of 2004 was particularly difficult for me because Annie was in the hospital for most of it, and my mind
and heart were not completely focused on other people's
kids. But I was determined that every child would have a
jolly-old-Saint-Nick moment no matter what.

One evening I had just come back from a break
and hadn't yet sat down when a woman approached me
and said, "I've been bringing my daughter to see you
for fourteen years. She was six when we came the first
time." She gestured to a lovely young lady. I shook her
hand, and then she hugged me. Her mom said, "She has
a surprise for you." The young lady hustled off the set
and around the corner. I decided to keep standing and
see what happened.

In a moment she came back—carrying a baby! She
walked up, handed me the newborn girl and said, "I
wanted my baby to come see my Santa for her first Santa

pictures." She didn't know I was already an emotional wreck, but she found out when I completely lost it, posing for a picture with Mom and Grandma, then carring the little one to the throne and letting them take a whole bunch of pictures. This was my first second-generation visit. I was bawling like a baby myself, and the one I was holding was looking quizzically at me. I could just hear her thinking, "What's the matter, Big Boy?" I am sure her family was asking the same question. I handed the baby back to Mom and thanked her. I truly was grateful she came.

That was my only second-generationer until a year later, when virtually the same scene played out again. This grandma also told me she first brought her daughter to see Santa when she was six, and that their family had repeated the event every year for fifteen years. She said she had an 8 by 10 print of every year's picture. They were framed and on the wall of their main hallway all year round. She was very excited about having a new picture with the mother and the grandbaby together.

After that shot, Mom gathered their other two kids and Dad, and we did a family portrait again. Mom was kind enough to say that I looked exactly the same in every one of their annual pictures. I told her that I was already old when she started saving them.

This time I did maintain control during the sweet moment. It just isn't proper for Santa to cry like a baby!

----------- DIARY TWO -----------

sharing *joy*

## EDUCATING SANTA

One of my longstanding personal rules has been that I never be seen in public with another Santa. I have walked out of many stores and restaurants when I've spotted another Santa there, because I don't want to cause the kids who might see us any trauma.

But at the same time, I've heard about a place in Midland, Michigan, that holds a Santa training school each year. At first, the idea of being with a group of Santas just didn't fit into my preconceived ideas of portraying the role. I found myself wanting to learn what was being taught there, but not wanting to be seen with a crowd of white-bearded wonders.

My book, TV appearances, and local and national newspaper articles had brought me letters and e-mails from Santas all over the country. In the summer of 2003, I received a call from a local guy named Gary Casey. He told me that a nationally known Santa from California was coming to Atlanta in September to conduct a one-day seminar for Santas. When I heard this, I decided I would bite the bullet and go.

It was a tremendous experience. Even after fourteen years of being Santa, I still learned a lot and met a bunch of terrific guys. The speaker was Tim Connaghan, a delightful guy filled with energy, love for the Lord, and an earnestness that was infectious to all seventy Santas and Mrs. Clauses in attendance. Because he'd read my book, Tim invited me to do a twenty-minute presentation on the real meaning of Christmas. It was an opportunity for me to talk about the Lord to all those Santas, and encourage them to use every chance they got to tell kids and adults about the roots of Santa history and the true meaning of Christmas.

Tim gave his seminar the audacious name of "International University of Santa Claus" and conferred the degree of "Bachelor of Clausology" on each graduate. I enjoyed it so much that I decided to go back the next year and to apply to the Michigan Santa School when I had the chance. I did Tim's seminar again, with Annie, in

September of 2004. She was not really well enough to go, but she didn't want to disappoint me. We had a good time together, and she learned a lot about how to improve her portrayal of Mrs. Claus. She was really tickled when she got her "Bachelor of Mrs. Clausology" degree. She called the whole day a "real hoot."

Soon after that, Annie's health went sour, and I spent my time taking care of her. I forgot all about the Santa School in Michigan. The summer of 2005, after Annie had died, I was beginning to come back to life myself when a Santa friend in High Point, North Carolina, called to remind me about the Michigan school. I applied immediately and started planning the trip.

Octobers in Michigan, I was to learn, can be spectacularly beautiful and unexpectedly cool. It was a little of both for the three days at the Charles W. Howard Santa School. But the cooler northern weather was made completely bearable by the warmth of the crowd of 100 students and the wonderful hospitality of the school dean, Tom Valent, and his wife, Holly, who served as registrar. They had assembled a formidable array of speakers and entertainers.

In no time at all, they had orchestrated a warm camarade-rie among all these look-alikes. We stood and sang songs to greet each speaker, then sang again to thank them when they finished. There could not have been a happier, more enthusiastic crowd. I learned a lot. Maybe not so much about how to be Santa as what a wonderful group of men and women were portraying the roles. There wasn't a grouch or a grinch anywhere to be found.

Charles W. Howard was the original Macy's store and parade Santa. He set such a high standard of performance excellence that other Santas sought him out for training and advice. He decided to start a school to train men who aspired to the role. His first class was in 1947. He passed the mantle of leadership to Tom and Holly Valent in 1997, and they moved the school to the charming little town of Midland, Michigan, where they built a wonderful site for the school downtown. Their Santa House is open for tours year round, and it's the site of the town's annual Christ-mas program. Every kid for miles around knows that San-ta comes to the Santa House to take orders for Christmas gifts each year.

We Santas were all over the little town of Midland. I discovered that nearly all the residents knew about the school and looked forward to the week when "class" was in session and the town was full of Santas. We went on field trips to several places. Noteworthy among them were the town of Frankenmuth and Bronner's, "The World's Largest Christmas Store."

We virtually took over the large dining room in a Bavarian-style restaurant in town. The other diners, kids included, seemed enchanted by the sight of so many Santas in one place. While we waited for our food, we broke into song and sang several of our favorites, completely captivating our involuntary audience. After the meal, we wandered in small groups around the town. We had so much fun in the shops and on the street that all my anxiety of being with a group of Santas melted away. I finally relaxed, went with the flow, and found myself having an absolutely wonderful time.

I was strolling down the sidewalk with three other Santas when a little guy came up to me, pointed, and said, "I think you are the real one."

I couldn't resist and responded, "Why do you think so?"

He said, "You just look more real than the rest of them."

He had no idea what a huge compliment he had just given me. I leaned over, put my index finger to my lips and, looking furtively up and down the sidewalk, said, "Shhh! Don't tell anybody, okay? It has to be a secret."

He said, "Okay!" and hustled back to his parents waiting farther down the sidewalk. I heard him shout to them as he ran, "I told you it was him, Mom." It had worked again. I never answered him directly, yet sent him on his way convinced of his answer. His faith and trust were restored, if they had ever even wavered. I could see that being with a group of Santas did not detract from the opportunity to share God's love. It may have even enhanced it.

The trip to Bronner's was completely awe-inspiring. There were more than four acres of merchandise—all Christmas, and mostly religious. I was in Santa heaven! With that many Santas in the store, it was not a surprise that there was a festive air. Everyone was having a wonderful time, probably me most of all. We were there for only an hour and a half—just enough time for me to grab a massive pile of Christmas stuff off the shelves and arrange for it to be shipped home. I had to swallow hard when I handed my credit card to the clerk and she announced, "That will be $352.80." Ouch! But there was no way I could put any of it back.

One of the Santas gave his business card to one of the kids, and in a flash there were crowds of kids dashing all through the store, asking the Santas for cards and collecting them by the handful. Unfortunately, I had only a few cards with me. One girl rushed up to me and said, "Gimme one of your cards!" I told her I didn't have any more. She demanded, "Why not?" When I told her I had given them all away, she angrily said, "Well, next time bring more!" Good advice.

Two other cardless Santas and I decided to sit down in a traffic-free spot. We were talking when a little girl named Christina came up to us holding a card. She started comparing our faces with the one on the card. One of the guys asked what she was doing, and she said, "I am searching for the real Santa. This is his picture."

When she turned the picture around, it was me! She

was holding my card! She placed the card in front of me and compared the picture and the faces. When she held the card up to me, she screamed. "That's him! I found him! This is the real Santa!"

If you love Christmas and are ever in Michigan, don't miss Bronner's. If you are not in Michigan, go there. It's worth the trip.

## SANTA CONVENTION

The event in Michigan doesn't constitute the biggest crowd of Santas I would ever be a part of. Years ago, Tim Connaghan, the seminar speaker, assembled a few Santas for a social event in California. He chartered the group with the highfalutin title of "Amalgamated Order of Real Bearded Santas" (AORBS). Later he opened the group to national membership, then decided to conduct an international convention in Branson, Missouri, in the summer of 2006.

It was a massive undertaking, which he began by recruiting volunteers to serve in various capacities on the convention committee. Cliff Snider, my Santa friend in High Point, asked me to help him on the committee managing vendor participation. That was a piece of cake for me, as I had a lot of experience with trade shows. Cliff and I struck a deal. He would keep up with the vendors and their requirements. I would deal with the hotel, prepare the rooms for the vendors, help them get set up on the day before the convention, and support them during the four days.

I drove out to Branson on July 4. I had recruited Dewaine Fisher, a rookie Santa from far north Georgia, as my copilot. The drive out there was easier than either of us thought. There was minimal traffic on the interstate. And we did have some fun encounters in a couple of restaurants and gas stations, as people wondered about this old Santa and his obviously younger sidekick. We told them he was my protégé.

The vendor setup went really well, and that spirit of Santa camaraderie appeared right away. I kept checking with the registration desk for attendance numbers, which topped out at almost 400 Santas—the largest gathering of real-bearded Santas ever assembled in one place. One fun part for me was that a very large number of them were bald, wore glasses, and generally looked a lot like me. One of them was a dead ringer. When I first looked at him, I thought I was looking into a mirror. Is that scary or what? I'll tell you how scary it was. I was standing in the lobby and a nice-looking lady came up to me, grabbed my arm, and said, "Come on, we're going to miss the bus." When I hesitated, she turned, studied me for a moment, then said, "Oh no, you're not my husband!"

I answered quickly, "Yeah, I know, but which bus are we going on?"

Very early on Friday morning, the entire crowd of Santas and Mrs. Clauses gathered for a parade in a shopping area a block from the hotel. More than 400 people showed up in red uniforms. The parade was timed for the network morning news shows, and some of the crews were there. We gathered behind the shopping area and, on signal, walked to the front and packed into a small courtyard. Several photographers and videographers were posted on a lift device high above us, and we stood around while they filmed and taped us. The results were quite a sight to behold. I wound up in the very back of the crowd and did not make it into any of the pictures that were printed and offered for sale. But it was a huge kick, and if there were any vestiges of my phobia about being in the company of other Santas, they were sure gone now!

Two people showed up in something other than Santa red that day, and one of them was my friend Cliff. He wore an authentic replica of the stars-and-stripes suit that first appeared in Thomas Nast cartoons in the early 1800s. The other was a Santa from Pennsylvania, a history buff who wore a replica of an early European version of a Sinter Klaas outfit. I found out that you actually can stand out in a crowd of Santa Clauses.

We had lots of classes in various Santa areas of interest—costuming, hair care, and dealing with difficult children and parents. We were able to attend five of the famous Branson entertainer shows, and every one of them was a spectacular experience. Santas were everywhere. We had such a good time. A group of us was eating in a restaurant when a mother came by and thanked us for being there. She said her two boys had stopped fussing when we came in—and had been good the whole time. They had decided that they needed to be on their best behavior for so many Santas.

One grown man in his early fifties stopped at our table, looked at me, and declared, "I am still disappointed that I did not get the car I asked for last Christmas."

I stood up and said, "Oh no, did I forget that? I'm sorry. Here, you can have it now." I pulled a toy car out of my pocket and handed it to him. He was stunned, and stood for a moment looking at the matchbox-sized vehicle. Then he said, "I wanted one I could ride in."

"Well," I retorted, "I am a toy maker, not an automobile manufacturer. I don't make cars you can ride in."

"Oh," he answered, handing me back the toy. "Give this to a kid who will enjoy it." He broke into a huge smile as he stuck out his hand and said, "Thank you so much; this was a fun moment. Thank you."

I shook his hand, and he went on his way. Adults can have fun encounters with Santa, too!

Several people armed with cameras followed us around as they "covered the event." One of them was a tiny lady with a video camera, and I began to realize that she was taking a lot of footage of me. I finally confronted her. She said she was from Voice of America, and she had asked Tim for an example of a Santa who best exemplified what Santa was all about. He told her about me and my ministry and history, and referred her to my Web sites. She was doing a mini documentary about me and promised she would let me see what she did with the footage.

The convention closed on Sunday at noon, and Tim had decided we needed to have a "church service" to close it out. I quickly agreed when he asked me if I would lead the service. I never pass up an opportunity to make an appeal for Santas to always remember that they are representing a man of God, Bishop Nicholas of Myra, and are ultimately representing our Lord and Savior, Jesus Christ. I reminded them that Jesus had been asked what the greatest commandment is, and that he had answered, "Love the Lord your God with all your heart, soul, mind, and strength." He had continued by saying, "and the second commandment, equal to the first, is to love your neighbor as yourself." That is our role as Santas: to emulate the love that Christ showed us and to pass it on to every child and adult we meet. I told my audience that if they had a problem with that, they should shave their beards and turn in their red suits, because that is what being Santa is all about. It is all about love.

## A LOST SLEIGH

After the Branson convention, I stayed in town for two extra days to sign books in a charming Christmas shop there. I also visited Silver Dollar City, a sister amusement park to my own Stone Mountain back home. We didn't have a lot of time, but we used it well. Dewaine, a fellow Santa, rode the roller coasters over and over while I wandered around the shops and outdoor shows. I did ride the train—to explore the differences between that one and the one back home.

Late in the afternoon, we saw a huge black cloud approaching and hustled for the exit. We made it there before the rain, but there were only three shuttle buses to take all the visitors to their cars. Suddenly the downpour was upon us. We huddled under my golf umbrella and waited through several cycles of buses. Finally we scrambled aboard. But we got very wet in the open-sided trams. Then, to my horror, I could not remember where I had parked the car. I knew which lot it was in, but I saw nothing that looked familiar. I let Dewaine use the umbrella and I struck out in the most driving rain I had ever experienced. I was soaked to the drawers in moments, and wetter than I ever was during the monsoon seasons in Vietnam. I wandered around for twenty minutes and never found my car. Several people tried to be helpful as they drove by. Others lowered their windows a sliver and shouted things like, "What happened, Santa, lose your sleigh?" Or, "Did your reindeer take off without you?" I did not respond with what I wanted to say, believe me. After all, what was that I just said about showing Christian love to all?

I finally went back to the shelter, where Dewaine was waiting, and he took off to look. Earlier, I had dropped him at the entrance and parked the car myself, but he found it in just a few minutes—barely 50 yards away from the shelter, but in the opposite direction.

There was a lesson here for Santa: always remember where you park your sleigh! It was also a reminder that I really am not Santa Claus, just an ordinary man with ordinary foibles.

A couple of weeks after the convention, I got an e-mail

from Tim with a link to Voice of America. I clicked on the site and was able to see what the little lady had done with the documentary. She had done a beautiful job of editing the footage, and the narration described a person I would really like to be. I was floored. But I was even more stunned when I found that it was being broadcast in more than forty countries around the world—and had been translated into nearly twenty languages! I could not help but think that here was this country boy from down a dirt road in North Carolina, and his story was being told all around the world. My mama would have been so proud! It was a very humbling experience. It also reminded me of a favorite line from Yakov Smirnoff, whose stand-up show we'd just seen in Branson. "What a country!"

I would attend Santa Tim's seminar again. And I will go to the convention again when it is held in 2008. I think the biggest lesson I have learned is that the Santa population in general is made up of kind, loving, caring men and women who show the love of the Lord to every kid they meet, on or off the throne.

## FESTIVALS AND
## CRAFT SHOWS

Any time I am out in public, I must be prepared to either
be Santa or reject the role. Although I am well aware of
this, I am often reminded that I am onstage and must be
ready to perform when needed.

I went with some friends to the Milford Memories
celebration in downtown Milford, Michigan. The town
closes off several blocks, and craftspeople and art-
ists set up tents to sell their wares. There are also food
booths, entertainers, and large crowds. As we made our
way among the tents, several of the vendors called me
Santa and made other comments. Several people posed
the most popular question: "Has anybody ever told you
that you look like Santa Claus?" Here I am, in a full white
beard and a red shirt with "Santa" embroidered above
the pocket. I restrained myself from answering, "Well,
duh!" I just chose to play dumb and say, "Really? You
think so? How about that!"

Some asked, "What are you doing here, Santa?" Answer: "I've got to vacation somewhere!" Another answer: "I'm checking my list. This is a great place to see if kids are being good boys and girls."

Others asked, "Who is making the toys, Santa?" Answer: "The elves have everything under control. I trained them well, so I don't have to be there all the time."

Many people just waved and said, "Hi, Santa." I waved back and said "Hello" or "Hi, there" or something equally as creative.

At one point I felt a tug on the back of my shirt. I turned around and saw three young boys looking expectantly at me. The biggest one stepped closer and said, "Are you Santa Claus?"

I leaned over to them and said, "No, I am the Easter Bunny."

"No you're not!" came the three-part-harmony reply.

"Oh, why not?" I asked.

"You just don't look like the Easter Bunny," the oldest retorted.

"Really? Who do I look like?" I leaned forward again.

"You look like Santa Claus," the oldest answered.

I leaned even closer to them, bringing my finger to my lips, and said, "Shhhh, don't tell anybody. Okay? I am on vacation."

They all nodded vigorously and disappeared into the crowd.

A few moments later, I felt another tug. The smallest of the three was standing there. I leaned forward as he raised his hand up to his cheek, looked around, and said confidentially, "Can I just tell my dad?"

"Okay, sure. You can tell your dad," I answered. He whirled around and was gone.

I never go to one of these events without trying some of the food. At Milford, it was the roasted corn on the cob that caught my eye, and I absolutely loved the taste of it. I knew there would be little chance of having that again, so I did what any red-blooded Santa would do. I ate another one.

There was a troop of Civil War re-enactors camped out in a meadow near the craft tents, and we walked over to see their encampment. They were well-established, with well-equipped and authentic tents, cooking gear, and accessories. The wives, children, and camp followers were there, too. The women were cooking the next meal while the men practiced drilling and tactical maneuvering. We spent some time talking with the women about life in the camp. They stayed in character as they described their activities.

None of them said a word about Santa or Christmas for a while, but then one of them noted, "We have Santa in our lives, too." I remembered from my history that Santa became an important figure just before the Civil War, when Clement Clark Moore wrote "A Visit from Saint Nicholas." The woman went on to tell me that they have an encampment at Christmastime, and one of their members dresses in an authentic period Santa outfit and plays the role for all the kids and families. It reminded me that Santa has been around a long time, and that even in those worst of days and conditions, he provided a measure of happiness for those fighting that miserable war.

We continued to wander around the fair for a while, and then left to get some real food. We settled into a booth and immediately caught the attention of two siblings sitting nearby. They stared. I waved. They waved back, and seemed completely absorbed by what they saw. In a few minutes, their dad went to the men's room. I gave him a moment, then went myself. I asked him his kids' names, and he told me: Katie and Brian. I went back into the dining room.

As I passed their booth, I stopped and asked the young lad, "Have you been good to your sister, Brian?"

The sister jumped and exclaimed, "He knows your name, Brian!"

I turned to her and said, "Of course I know his name, Katie. I know a lot of things. Like I know you have been picking on Brian some, too."

Her mouth flew open and her eyes grew wide.

"That is why you have to always be a good girl, Katie, and a good boy, Brian. You just never know who is watching you. Okay, can you remember that?"

They both nodded sheepishly.

"Good. Keep it up." And I went to my seat.

The family left before we did, and as they went by our booth they each told me goodbye. It occurred to me that they will have quite a story to tell their grandchildren!

## GRANDPA SANTA

Speaking of grandchildren, folks ask me from time to time what my own grandchildren think about having Santa as a grandpa. I do have grandchildren—five of them. They range in age from four to twenty-one. Joshua, the twenty-one-year-old and his nineteen-year-old sister, Jessica, carry my picture card with them and love to tell their friends about me. They report that most of their friends simply don't believe that the guy in the picture is their Gramps. They have a different last name, so the words on the back of my card don't mean much to their friends.

Eleven-year-old Kristen and nine-year-old Taylor have a lot of fun trying to convince their friends that their grandpa is Santa, a fact they believe with all their hearts. Sometimes I show up at the sports events where they are cheerleaders and add some credibility to their claims. They seem to love it.

Then there is Logan, only four and still trying to decide

what she believes. Sometimes one of the grandkids will ask me the dreaded question, "Are you really Santa Claus, Grandpa?" I answer the same way I answer other kids. I say, "Don't you tell anybody, okay? It has to be a secret."

I am also the father of three boys and one girl. Paul, the oldest, is now a dead ringer for his old man. In a year or so he will be a great Santa in his own right. When he was a little guy, his favorite thing was to ride through the neighborhood where we were living in Kailua, Hawaii, and see all the Christmas lights. He would stand in the back seat of the car, peering out the windows and pointing, saying, "Yook at the yights, Dad. Yook at the yights, Mom!" He would get so excited.

When Mark, my second son, was about three, he became an amateur mechanic and professional snoop. He could not stand seeing a closed door, drawer, or box. He HAD to open it to see what was inside. He would never mess with what he found. Once he had seen it, he would quietly close the lid or door and leave it alone. When we would visit friends or family, he always drove our hosts crazy by snooping through things. My older brother's wife would follow him around, trying to herd him back to where the people were. But he would just go back to where he had left off and continue snooping.

He also loved to take things apart and see how they worked. He disassembled just about everything he could get his hands on. One year as Christmas approached, I told him that if he kept breaking things, Santa was going to bring him a brick, a concrete block, and a two-by-four. I told him that a few times, and then a couple of weeks later, I took him to see Santa at the mall. When it was his turn, he jumped up on Santa's lap and, when he was asked the expected question, responded, "I want a brick, a concrete block, and a two-by-four." The look on Santa's face was classic.

On Christmas morning, I made sure Mark got what he had asked for. I wrapped up a brick, a concrete block, and a two-foot length of two-by-four. When he came down from his bedroom, he ran to the tree, picked up the brick, and started to unwrap it. He dropped it before he finished unwrapping it, and it broke in two. When he tried to pick up the concrete block, he dropped it and it broke, too. He was able to unwrap the two-by-four without breaking it. Of course, there were also toys, stuffed animals, and a couple of games. But he was really sad and disappointed that what he had really wanted had broken. (But so did the rest of his gifts, within a couple of weeks.)

## ---------- HERE COMES SANTA CLAUS ----------

"The Grand Entrance of Santa Claus" has become a nightly feature at Stone Mountain Park. We call it the Parade, since all the characters performing in the various shows precede the sleigh for the walk through our replica village of Crossroads.

The sleigh is made of plywood attached to one of the Kawasaki work carts used by the maintenance crew—a valiant attempt at a replica sleigh. It is painted red and white and trimmed with gold filigree. The sleigh is outlined and covered with lights. Out in front of the sleigh is a pair of metal beams that support five of those white lawn reindeer that are filled with lights and whose heads move either from side to side or up and down. The lights on this incredible operation are illuminated via a gas-powered generator mounted underneath the sleigh's wooden frame. It is loud and smells of burning motor oil. One of our characters, dressed in an elf outfit, drives while Santa stands, supported by the high sides of the sleigh.

The parade starts at the Great Barn and travels down the main street of Crossroads which, even on the worst of weather days, is lined with a crowd of adoring spectators awaiting a glimpse of the jolly old elf. We get a big kick out of waving and shouting "Merry Christmas" to folks along the route. The view of the millions of lights in the village is quite spectacular from up in the sleigh. I absolutely love that sight, so it's easy to be jolly.

Most nights there's at least one Santa heckler in the crowd. Comments like, "Happy Holidays, not Merry Christmas, Santa!" are not uncommon. If I answer at all, I usually say, "In Crossroads, it is Merry Christmas!" Occasionally some smart aleck will comment about the reindeer: "Your reindeer are getting skinny, Santa. You need to feed them better." My best response to that is, "They are being fed 110 volts AC at 60 amps. That's all they need."

But that is not always true. Sometimes the cantankerous generator will shut down, cutting power to the lights on the sleigh and reindeer. If it won't start after a few tries, we just make the trip in the dark. That brings on another round of heckling. But it is all in fun and we enjoy that, too. It breaks up the routine for sure.

Everybody knows there are "eight tiny reindeer," plus Rudolph. I just told you we have five. The front one has a red bulb on his nose, so everyone knows who he is. We get a lot of comments about missing reindeer. I can't tell folks that we initially tried longer beams with nine reindeer, but their weight stuck out so far that the rear wheels of the sleigh lifted off the ground. And when we ballasted it to keep them down, the length made it very tricky to steer down the narrow streets of town. We compromised with five. Sometimes, reality takes priority over fantasy.

One of my favorite appearances is my annual trip to High Point. I have made some great friends there, just by seeing the kids and parents for a few minutes once a year.

On my most recent visit, I was invited to have dinner at the home of a dentist, Joel Gentry, and his wife, Shirene. This was the sixth time they had extended that courtesy. Shirene asked me in advance what I would like to eat, and I told her very truthfully that I had learned that anything she put on her table was delicious. As long as there was no liver, sugar, or trans-fats, I would love it. The Gentrys showed me a photo album that documents the "Santa visits" of their sons, Austin and Forrest, from the time they were infants. Austin was a newborn the first time I saw him. Now he is a strapping, handsome fourteen-year-old. The last time I dined with the Gentrys, he was going to a school dance and was very excited. As I studied the album, I could see that I really don't look like I have aged. I told

Shirene it must be because of my genes!

Another family I enjoy visiting is Bob and Sandra Wilkinson's. For the past several years, they have taken me out to dinner at a seafood restaurant. I can count on a lot of laughter around the table as we catch up on events in our lives during the preceding year. This last time, though, we discussed a somber subject as they told me about Sandra's battle with cancer. She is doing well and is very optimistic, praising the Lord for His hand in her treatment.

We always have a great time interacting with the other patrons at the restaurant. It isn't every day that you see an authentic-looking Santa in his full regalia, sitting at the next table as you dine. At least in that outfit no one tells me, "Hey, you like Santa Claus!" This time several people brought their kids by to see me, and some even filmed the moment. One mother said, "Thanks, Santa, you just saved us a trip to the mall to get that picture."

The food was wonderful, and the fellowship and en-counters were even more wonderful. The Wilkinson grandchildren, Drew and Riley, have grown up having supper with Santa one night a year. Those kids are delightful and beautiful. Riley is five this year, and his dimpled cheeks are becoming more prominent. He told me that a girl in his class told the teacher that he has holes in his cheeks and is so cute! He really is cute, and she will not be the last girl who will think so.

I don't usually include stories that don't happen to me personally, but this one is just too precious to pass up. In the course of the evening, Bob told me about a four-year-old boy who was taken to see another Santa. When the Santa asked him what he wanted for Christmas, the boy hesitated a few moments before blurting out, "A bug zapper!" Santa looked at his parents, but they had no explanation for this request.

The first time I saw her, she was struggling to walk to me. She was dragging one foot, and one arm was drawn up tight to her side. It was 2002. She was five, but she was small for her age. I helped her up onto my lap. She snuggled tight against me and laid her head on my shoulder. She sighed heavily, and I was sure it was because she was worn out from the exertion of walking. I said hello and asked how she was doing. She answered, "Better now."

I asked her what was going on. She slowly answered, "I have a brain tumor, Santa. I've already had two surgeries and I have more to go, then I'll be well."

My heart nearly stopped. How could this beautiful child be dealing with such a terrible subject so simply and confidently? I hugged her closer and responded, "Tell me your name, sweetie."

"My name is Kylie, Santa."

"I am going to be praying for you, Kylie. In fact, let's

pray right now." I bowed my head and she put her forehead against my cheek. I prayed a prayer of contrition and petition of healing for this lovely child. I felt like I didn't want to stop praying, but knew I could not keep it up forever. I was speaking quietly so only Kylie and I could hear my voice, but I knew that the words were reaching the ears of the One who needed to hear them.

While I was praying, Kylie's grandmother took a picture of us. I did not know it had happened and when I opened my eyes, Kylie's grandmother was not there. Kylie told me her list and as she did, her grandmother came back into the store. Kylie's little brother Connor, who obviously adores his sister, and their cousin Brittany, who adores both of them, had been patiently waiting. There were some other kids in line, too. So I finally had to let Kylie go on her way. I kept my promise and prayed for her often over the next year.

Annie went with me for the next visit. It was in a children's clothing store called Tadpoles, a new venue for me. I was afraid Kylie's family would not hear about the new place and may not make it.

At one point I was concentrating on a boy sitting on my left leg, and was aware that Annie was interacting with someone on the bench to my right. I let the little fellow down and he toddled off. Then Annie said, "Here is Kylie, Santa." I turned and my eyes watered. She looked terrific. Her color was better, and she had grown a lot and gained some weight. I hugged her and Annie, too, so tightly I nearly melted them together. I looked at her grandmother, a delightfully loving woman named Angie Bean. She was grinning broadly and nodding her head vigorously. "Does this mean what I think it means, Gran?" I asked.

She said, "Yes it does, Santa. Kylie is doing much, much better! The tumor is benign and most of it is gone now. She is relearning a few things, but she is much better." She also handed me an 8 by 10 print of the photo she took a year earlier, of Kylie and me praying together. It is now the most treasured of all the photos in my album.

More tears rolled down my face and I shouted "Praise the Lord!" for all to hear and hugged everybody again, Gran included. I promised to keep praying for Kylie and told her granny to keep me posted by e-mail.

2005 was an agonizing year, but although it hurt to go to High Point without Annie, a promise is a promise. This time when Kylie came in the door I saw that huge smile immediately. I got out of my chair and walked to her to give her a hug. Then we walked together back to the chair. She gave me a full report, and her Gran confirmed it. Kylie was still improving and her speech was much better. She told me she was being monitored periodically, and everything was going well. Her walking had improved more, although she still had a bit of a limp. She told me she was sorry about Annie. I told her that now we both had an angel in heaven looking out for us. She liked that idea.

Another year passed. Now Kylie is ten and becoming a lovely young lady. I am not sure how many more years I will be able to go to High Point, but Kylie will always be in my prayers. I am sure I will get reports from Granny Angie from time to time. I have always known that prayer works. But to see a walking testimony to its power is an awesome thing. And to have been a part of it is a humbling experience. Thank you, Lord, for using me to bring joy and happiness to this wonderful little girl and her family.

## A NEW VENUE

I am new to the Hill Skills Crafts and Art Exhibition in Greenville, South Carolina. It is hosted by a lady named Rachel McKaughan, who was raised just a mile away from us when we lived in Guilford County, North Carolina. We had not seen each other in over fifty years. My brother Peter had been in touch with her, and he told her I was a published author. She told him she needed an author for this year's show, and when I found out, I decided to go for at least part of the four-day session. I did the appearance in my Santa suit, and had a tremendous time signing books and having my picture taken with visitors.

I was not swamped with customers, so I spent some time touring the booths and passing out brochures for my book. People were quite surprised to see Santa aimlessly walking around the place, while I was shocked by the quality of the offerings of the crafters. I tried my best to resist buying some things, but finally did succumb to temptation and bought a couple of Santa artifacts to add to my collection.

In the booth next to mine there was a nice lady selling potted orchids. I have always been fascinated by those beautiful flowers, and was able to work a trade with her: one orchid for one of my books. She started to read the book right away. As the day wore on, I could hear her chuckling, laughing, and even crying out loud. It looked like she hated to stop reading to wait on customers. I considered it a big endorsement for my writing.

When I got the orchid home, I did my best to follow the woman's instructions. But like most plants I have ever had, I managed to kill it off in just a few months.

Another great craft show is the annual Yellow Daisy Arts and Crafts Festival. It takes place the weekend after Labor Day, and has been a Stone Mountain Park tradition for over twenty-five years. There are over 400 crafters there and a careful gleaning process has selected the very best of the nearly 1,000 artisans who apply, so the quality of the products is a wonder to behold. The booths are spread along paved pathways in the woods and the stroll among the booths is an absolute delight. I try to go every year.

If I really want to get into the fun, I put on a red shirt and groom my beard. Most crafters are garrulous by nature and I am constantly greeted with, "Hi, Santa!" The shoppers are usually more surprised to see me, and often do double takes. Many smile broadly and nod in recognition. Many greet me with comments like, "Where are your reindeer?" or "How are things going at the Pole?"

Of course these questions are not new to me, and I'm always well-prepared. "The reindeer are at the North Pole; it is much too hot here for them this time of year." Or "Things are going great at the North Pole. Pete, the chief Elf, is in charge. We did have a slight slowdown on the Barbie line yesterday, but today we're back to full production."

And of course there is always someone who asks, "Has anyone ever told you that you look like Santa Claus?"


I have already introduced Pete, the patriarch of a family of little people who "elf" for me every night at Stone Mountain Park. He sits beside me in his little chair, and we keep a running dialogue going between kids. His interaction with the kids and families is fun for me to watch. He is also the receptionist at my ministry, Friends of Disabled Adults and Children.

Many families tell us they have been coming for ten or fifteen years. Pete's usual response is, "Wow, I was just a little guy back then, wasn't I?" Most times folks don't know how to respond to that, since he is only three feet, nine inches tall and has been that size for fifty years. Pete loves it.

His wife, Mary Alice, and his children, Bunny, Heidi, and Trent, have also "elfed" for me from time to time. They are all a delightful bunch. At least once a year, they all show up at the park with some of their friends and their friends' children, all little people. The "big people" there usually can't believe their eyes as the whole place is full of little people. We all have a lot of fun with the various reactions. But I'll talk more about that later.

Another special day for me is the annual "Breakfast with Santa" fundraising event for Friends of Disabled Adults and Children. It is a huge kick to walk into a room of 250 people and watch them react to my sudden appearance in the doorway. Pete brings some of his kids, their spouses and their kids, and they all help pass out the few hundred toys we have accumulated for this event. Trent's five-year-old son, Jonah, was a big hit at the 2005 breakfast. He was having a tremendous time rushing around to find toys for each child on my lap. It was a true joy to watch him. He went home and told his two shy sisters all about it. A week later, they came to the park and, for the first time, ran right to me and sat on my lap without hesitation.

## ----------- TYPICAL ENCOUNTERS -----------

I love encounters that happen in public places when I least expect it! For instance, I was eating in a Golden Corral restaurant in Marietta, Georgia. We were having a spirited evening. I was wearing black trousers and a red knit shirt. The other couple had not met me before that night, and they seemed intrigued with the whole Santa persona. When I went to the buffet, they would follow along behind me and watch how people reacted to having Santa among them.

We were in the middle of our meal when I felt a tap on my left shoulder. I turned to see a beautiful little girl of about six. She had a hesitant, apprehensive look on her wide-eyed face. I smiled and said, "Hello, Sweetie. How are you?"

She ignored my question and blurted out the question she had been holding back. "Are you Santa Claus?"

I have told you about this sequence before, but I enjoy

it, so let me repeat.

"No, Sweetie, I am the Easter Bunny."

"No, you aren't! You don't look like the Easter Bunny." She said this so forcefully that I knew I was not toying with just any little girl. This was a smart kid and I had better be on my toes.

"Oh, who do I look like?"

"You look like Santa Claus!"

Leaning forward, I raised my finger to my lips and said, "Shhh, don't tell anybody. It has to be a secret, okay?"

She raised her finger to her lips and, mimicking me, said in a near whisper, "Shhh, okay. I won't tell anybody." The expression on her face was so cute it took my breath away. She leaned toward me and said, "Can I tell my mom?" I nodded, and she took off to a table in the corner. Halfway across the restaurant, she shouted, "It *is* Santa Claus, Mom! I told you it was!"

In a few minutes she was back with another tap on my shoulder. "Where are your reindeer?"

"They're at the North Pole. It's much too warm here for reindeer today."

A quick nod and she was gone again.

She returned shortly. "Do you know what I want for Christmas?"

"No, I don't. Why don't you tell me?"

She elbowed her way between me and my friend, and when I slid my chair back, she pushed her way onto my lap (for she clearly knew where she had to be to give me her order). As she climbed, she began to give me her list. It started, in typical little girl fashion, with Barbies and a Baby Alive doll. Then she threw in an iPod, MP3 player, Xbox, Gameboy, Nintendo DS, and a couple of other electronic games. She finished up with a cell phone. Boy, she really was a sophisticated little girl. But these items could force her family into bankruptcy! I told her she had big list, and that and I would see what I could do about it, but not to count on all of that. She said she knew she wouldn't get it all.

This time when she ran back to her mom, I watched where she went. I discovered that her mother was a waitress in the restaurant, and wondered what kind of life they led. I found myself wishing I could just hand her a Gameboy or something. But my pockets were empty. All I had in there were some suckers and a couple of Matchbox cars.

The place I hold forth for most of the season is the throne at Stone Mountain Park. They move me around from year to year, from building to building, but the scene on the throne itself is almost always the same. One year they did make it more difficult than usual. The throne had a backdrop of four red bookcases that were filled with toys of all kinds. When I asked the kids what they wanted for Christmas, they spent a lot of time telling me the toys on the shelves were what their little hearts desired. Some even went so far as to say they wanted a red car or a yellow truck, both of which were prominently displayed. But at least I didn't have to sit there while they were trying to think of something to say. That is when I discovered that very few of the kids come ready to spout off a well-thought-out list of things they actually do want. Many times, when I ask the question, there is no answer at all—just a long pause as their minds go blank.

But sometimes the answers do give me something to

report to you.

And sometimes the answers will break your heart.

One special girl's story comes to mind. She looked like any of the thousands of kids who had sat on my lap. She was about seven, which is older than some. She was pleasant enough as I asked her how she was doing. It was when I asked the next question that a dark cloud came over her face. "What would you like for Christmas?" I asked.

She immediately responded, "All I want is for my family to be together for Christmas."

"And what would that take?" I asked.

"You have to get my mama out of jail."

The air went out of me involuntarily. But throwing caution to the wind, I decided to go on and ask, "Where is your dad?"

This time she sighed. "We don't know. He's been gone a long time."

"Well, who is taking care of you?" I felt so helpless.

"I'm living with my grandma; that's her over there." A lovely lady waved as the girl pointed to her. I could not even begin to fathom the pain her grandma must be feeling.

"Well, Sweetie, how about we pray for your mama and your daddy?"

"Now?"

"Sure, right now." So we did. I threw in a prayer for Grandma, too.

After I said amen, I gave her a big hug and told her, "Don't ever forget that God loves you and Santa loves you, too." And that was the absolute truth.

I have had several kids who told me that they wanted their dads to come home from Iraq. But I was not prepared for another little girl who told me she wanted her daddy and her mommy to come home.

"Both of them?" I blurted out.

"Yeah," she answered. "They're both in the National Guard and they both got called up. I am staying with my mom's sister and her kids."

"Are you all getting along?" Dumb question, Santa!

"Yeah, we are. It's kind of like going to your cousins' for a visit. But I miss my mom and dad. I e-mail them every day and tell them what's going on. But . . . I do miss them."

"Of course you miss them. I know they're proud of you

for being such a good girl about it, and I'm sure they're looking forward to your getting together again."

There was no dark cloud here, just a powerful good feeling about the whole situation. I am sure that was because of the sensitivity of her aunt and cousins and the encouragement of her parents, who weren't there in body, but certainly were in heart.

Sometimes it seems I have heard about everything I may ever hear from kids. And just when I'm beginning to think it's true, I am caught off guard again.

One little guy looked completely average. He was about six, blond, and very outgoing. He answered my first question with elaborate enthusiasm, "I am fine, doing good, being a good boy." I noticed that his mother had approached closer than parents usually do. I motioned her back a little to get her out of the picture, then as soon as the flash happened she moved in close again.

"Well then, what do you want for Christmas?"

This is the part that practically knocked me off the throne. He said, with that same enthusiasm, "I want a ghost!"

"Whoa, wait a minute," I responded. "Did you say you want a ghost?"

"Yeah, a ghost. That's all I want, a ghost."

I looked at Mom, and she was nodding.

"A ghost?" I said to her. The little guy hopped off my lap and took off for the craft area. His job was done. He had told me what he wanted.

Mom stepped up and said, "That's all he's talked about since he saw a movie a few months ago. He thinks a ghost will keep him company, help with his homework, and do all his chores."

"Well, good luck handling that one!" I responded.

"Yeah, thanks," she said over her shoulder as she moved toward the picture-ordering counter. A ghost, of all things. Good grief!

It is funny how closely kids are paying attention, and yet how much they miss. One little fellow was about five, and all business. He prefaced his list by saying, "At my mom's house I want you to bring . . ." and he continued with several items.

When he had finished I asked him, "And what do you want at your dad's house?"

"Oh, yeah. Thanks," he answered, then launched into a new list with different items. Then he said, "Okay, that's all." He hopped off my lap and was gone to his mom. They moved away to the crafts area, and a few moments later, Mom stepped up to me.

"How did you do that?" she asked.

"Do what?" I responded, completely puzzled by her query.

"My son just told me that you had to be the real Santa because you knew that his dad and I were divorced. How did you know that?"

I tapped my forehead and said, "Why are you surprised? You know I know everything."

She smiled a moment and then walked away.

That was no great magic, I was just listening and following the clues.

Another mother stepped up to me after her five-year-old had finished giving me his list and had moved off to his dad. She told me her older son could not make it that night, but that he wanted her to give me his list because he was absolutely convinced that I was the real Santa. I asked her why he was so convinced.

She said that the previous year he could not be there either, and he had told his little brother to tell me he wanted a hunting bow for Christmas. The little brother had done it and told his mom about it on the way home. That was the first time she had heard about a hunting bow. She talked to Dad, and they decided he was mature enough to be trusted with one. So on Christmas morning, he got his bow.

He was ecstatic. He asked the family, "How did Santa know I wanted a bow?"

His little brother said, "I told him you wanted one, like you told me to do."

Later, the big brother told his mom and dad, "I knew that Santa at Stone Mountain was the real one."

"And he made sure his friends heard that story, too." Mom said as she left.

I absolutely love doing the unexpected!

Once I noticed a particular mom and daughter communicating in sign language while they were waiting. I couldn't tell which one of them was deaf, but I thought it was the daughter—a young lady of about eight or nine.

As they were approaching the throne, I made the gesture for "I sign." Both their faces lit up. Maybe they were both deaf, I thought.

I seated the daughter on my lap and signed, "Are you a good girl?" She nodded vigorously.

Then I signed, "What do you want for Christmas?"

I do know the signs for some toys but she was flying through her list. I was barely able to keep up just agreeing with her. When she finished her list, she gave me a big hug and started to move away. Then she stopped and, looking over her shoulder, said, "Thanks, Santa." Then her mother rushed up to me, hugged my neck and kissed me on the cheek.

It was her mother who was deaf, and the girl had wanted her mom to know what she was asking for. I was so glad

I had the ability to make that happen.

Here's another funny one. I had heard from somebody that some kids really do like to work in the yard. Mine certainly never did, so I had a hard time believing it.

This kid looked like an ordinary six-year-old. When I asked him what he wanted for Christmas, I expected to hear an iPod, MP3 player, or Nintendo DS like all the other boys his age I'd seen so far. But his response was, "A leaf blower!"

"A leaf blower?" I responded.

"No, make that two leaf blowers," he answered.

"Two leaf blowers!" I was even more amazed.

"Yeah," he responded, quite matter-of-factly. "One for me and one for my brother so we can work in the yard at the same time."

"Of course, how silly of me!" I responded, chuckling. I looked at his mom and shrugged my shoulders.

She stepped forward and said, "That's the only thing he's talked about getting for months."

"Does he really work in the yard?" I inquired.

"Yes, he does. They both love to work in the yard. They would rather work outside than play outside."

"Wow, that's really something. Want to trade them?"

A smile, but no answer. It was worth a try, anyway.

People do ascribe a lot of magical powers to Santa Claus, but he definitely has his limits. One little boy's demeanor made me think he was troubled by something. He was less than exuberant about the walk to the throne and getting on my lap. Instead of asking what he wanted for Christmas, I almost asked him what was bothering him. But before I could say anything to him, he said, "There is only one thing I want for Christmas this year, Santa."

"And what would that be?" I asked.

"All I want is for my brother's diabetes to be cured. He doesn't deserve that."

"No, he doesn't deserve that," I answered. "Nobody deserves something like that. Nobody. But bad things do happen to good people, and there is no explanation for why that happens. One thing we can do is pray for him. Let's do that now."

My prayer was for the brother and for this little boy who loved him enough to give up his Christmas for him. Then I promised I would pray some more for both of them. I encouraged him to pray for his brother, too, and turned him loose. As he went away, his steps seemed a bit jauntier. I did not reveal to him that I'm a diabetic, too.

Another kid looked skeptical as he walked toward my throne. His arms were folded across his chest, and he seemed apprehensive. He stepped onto my stool and swung onto my left leg.

"My mama made me come here for a picture," he blurted. "I don't believe in you."

"Oh, you don't? Why don't you believe in me?"

"You got on a phony beard, that's why!"

Now I do work hard to make my beard look well groomed, but I never had anyone tell me it was phony before. And besides he hadn't really looked at it closely. I decided to take the kind approach. "Well, have you really looked at it?" I asked. At least he hadn't tried to snatch it off of me like a couple have.

He turned and looked at my face. He jumped perceptibly, and his face took on a new look. He turned his head back and forth as he looked, and then he almost shouted, "Wait, it really is growing right out of your face!"

I said, "Sure it is. That's what real beards do. They grow right out of your face."

This time he really did shout, "It is real! It's a real beard. He's the real Santa!" Then he jumped off my lap and started to walk away. Suddenly he whirled around and leaned toward me. "Now I do believe," he said confidentially. Then he walked away. A little while later, he came back and handed me his list without a word, just a big grin on his face.

I have always been something of a car nut, but I did not know that young kids can be car nuts, too.

This little fellow had bright, excited eyes as he climbed onto my lap. I didn't even have a chance to ask him my questions. He immediately launched into his list by saying, "I want cars, lots of them. I want a big race car set, a bunch of Matchbox cars, some remote control cars, and some NASCAR collectible race cars."

"Just cars, huh?" I finally got a word in.

"Yeah, and lots of them," he responded as he hopped down and walked away.

Another little guy had some real specifics in mind when he put in his requests. I should have had a clue when he came up wearing a Dale Earnhart, Jr. jacket and a Mark Martin baseball cap.

"I want only model NASCAR race cars. I already have some, but I want the rest of them, all in 1:18 scale."

"Who do you already have?" I asked, trying to be helpful.

"Well, let's see," he mused. "I already have Dale Junior, Mark Martin (Why did I know that already?), Kyle Petty, Kasey Kahne," and he went on to name several more. When he stopped with familiar names, he added, "There are some rookies coming along that don't have model cars out yet, but when they do come out, I want them."

Here was a man who was clearly devoted to his hobby. I couldn't help but wonder if he had caught that obsession from his parents. Things like that are often contagious. I looked into the crowd of observers, and sure enough, there was a couple who had on Dale Earnhart, Jr. jackets. Dad even had on a Mark Martin cap. Must run in the family, I guess!

Kids can sometimes get very specific. Like one young lady, who wanted to make sure I knew her name was Andie. She even spelled it out carefully so I would know it was not spelled like a boy's name.

Her first request was for some animals from the Littlest Pet Shop collection. She made sure I knew that part, then she gave me a list of animals: a dog, a cat, a kitten, a monkey and several other animals. When she finished, she said, "Okay, got that?"

I nodded and she went on.

"I want a train set with wooden tracks."

I nodded and said, "Like Thomas the Tank Engine trains?"

"Yeah," she brightened up even further, and went on to name several of the Thomas characters. "Make sure you include some bridges and trestles and buildings with the set, okay?"

She went on, "I want a big Fairytopia. A big one, not a

little one. Okay?"

I nodded again. I was not familiar with that one. This was the first request for that, so I made a mental note to check that out in the toy catalog.

I was getting curious about how long this could go on. "I want a butterfly doll set in pink. Got it?"

"Got it." I responded.

"And the last thing is …" Finally, the end is in sight, I thought. "I want a Dorothy wig from *The Wizard of Oz.*"

"So, you want to look like Dorothy, huh?"

"Yeah, she is so cute!"

"Yes, she is. Well, that is quite a specific list, and I will see what I can do to find all those things."

"Okay. Thank you," she said merrily, and ran to her parents.


Another guy had an obsession with motor vehicles. He told me, "I want some toy trucks. Lots of them. All kinds and sizes and colors."

"How many of them do you want?" I was searching for specifics.

"I want 500 of them," he said, "all sizes and colors and kinds of trucks."

"Is that all you want?" I queried.

"Yep, just trucks." Then he jumped off my lap.

He took two steps and turned around just as I was helping the next little girl up and said, "On second thought, don't make it that many. My dad can't count that high."

Sometimes some of the results of sibling conflict become visible to even a casual observer. I remember a little guy who looked like a fighter as he mounted my knee. As I helped him up, I felt a cast on his forearm. Checking it out, I found it went all the way up to his armpit. I asked him, "How did you break your arm?"

He answered, "My brother did it."

"What did he hit you with?" I asked.

"A baseball bat."

"A baseball bat! My goodness. Well, should I put him on the bad boy list?"

"No," he answered enthusiastically. "He didn't mean to. It was an accident. He was aiming at my head. I put my arm up and he hit that instead."

I saw another case of sibling conflict at the Atlanta RV show. I was touring through several Class A RVs parked outside and was followed on board a very nice unit by a mother and her brood of four boys. The oldest boy, about fourteen, came on right behind me and sat down in the driver's seat. His next brother came on and sat in the passenger seat. Mom came on next. She was well in when the third son, about eight or ten years old came up the steps.

This unit had the entry door right in front of the passenger seat. As the third boy went by his brother, the older boy stuck out his leg and tripped the younger one, sending him sprawling to the floor. I was looking right at them. Their mother was looking at the kitchen of the RV, but when she heard the crashing noise, she turned around. I said loudly, "I don't believe he did that—and right in front of me, too!" I reached into my back pocket for my day planner and opened it up. "I think he needs to go on my bad boy list for that little trick." Mom nodded to me.

"Oh, rats! I've lost my pen," I exclaimed.

Mom said, "I have one!" and instantly handed me the

one in her hand. I took it and asked her his name. "It's Dillon, Santa. You should remember him."

"Oh, yes I do. Let me make a note of this to add to his record." I wrote down a few words and handed the pen back to Mom. I thanked her and went on to finish my tour of the RV.

About a half hour later, in another part of the exhibit area, I saw the boys again. "Hello, Dillon," I said. "I hope you're being a good boy now." He nodded through a sheepish grin.

I hate shopping. I have always hated shopping. When I need something, I usually know exactly what it is, go to the store, buy it, and leave. And now, with my beard, shopping has gotten extremely difficult. Actually, I don't mind the Santa encounters. I truly enjoy them, but they do complicate the shopping that I already dread.

Let me describe my typical shopping trip by explaining the one I had just yesterday. I made sure I was not wearing any red clothes. I had on a green shirt, brown jacket, a blue FODAC baseball cap, black pants, and brown shoes. As I walked in the door the greeter immediately said, "Hello, Santa, welcome to Wal-Mart. Here is a cart for you and our latest ad. Toys are to your left in the far corner of the store." I smiled, said hello and waited while she finished her spiel, took the cart, and started toward the housewares department. I only went about fifty feet when I heard someone behind me say, "Ho, Ho, Ho! Hello, Santa."

I turned, and a large man with a scraggly salt and pepper goatee was standing by his cart, smiling at me. I smiled back and he said, "You have a lovely beard."

I said, "You could have one, too, if you quit trimming that fuzz on your face and let it grow on out."

He said, "I tried that once and it drove me crazy. How can you stand it?"

"I never think about it," I answered. "It's just part of me, and I never mess with it."

"Well, it sure does look good. You look like the real Santa."

"Thank you very much," I said, and meant every word of it.

I had almost made it to the housewares area when a manager came by and said, "Finding everything you're looking for, Santa?"

He helped me locate the five Rubbermaid sixty-six-gallon storage tubs I had come for.

I pushed my cart up to the checkout counter. The cashier looked up and said dryly, "Hello, Santa. Did you find everything you were looking for?"

"Yes, sure did," I answered, as she ran up the sale.

On my way out, the door hadn't even shut when I heard two small voices saying, "Hi Santa! Hi Santa! Hi Santa!" I saw two little guys of about eight or ten and gave them high fives as they went into the store with their mom.

Is that a typical shopping trip? Yeah, pretty much.

Here's another version. I was at Sam's Club and saw an older lady in an electric wheelchair. Her left leg was missing above the knee. When I got close enough, I could see that the chair had come from FODAC. It had one of our stickers on it—from at least eight years ago. There was a rush of pride and gratitude that God had used me and our ministry to help this lady. Our paths crossed a few times as we moved around the store, and finally, I could stand it no longer. "How is that chair running these days, Ma'am?"

"Good," she answered. "It's running real good, always has."

"How long have you had it?"

"Ten years. My son and I were just talking about that," she said, motioning to the younger man who was accompanying her.

"Oh yeah," he interjected. "You're the Santa from the wheelchair place, aren't you?"

"Yes, I am," I answered. "How did you know?"

"I've seen you on television and read about you in the paper."

"Well, how is your mama's chair working these days?"

"Fine," he answered. "She uses it all the time and it just keeps on going."

"I'm glad to hear that. And I'm glad that the Lord used us to help her through a difficult time."

"Well, you sure did that," he responded enthusiastically. "That chair has made a big difference in her life. Thank you so much for your help."

"You are certainly welcome. God bless you," I responded as I moved on.

I have done Santa at that store for the employees' children, and when I got to the checkout line, the clerk said, "Hey, Santa, how's it going?"

"Great!" I answered. "Absolutely supreme!" And I meant it.

# the greatest
# of these is *love*

## MY CHILDHOOD SANTA VISITS

People seem fascinated by how I came to look like this and portray the jolly fat guy. It does seem an unlikely outcome for a man who has been through all that I have. But it is not all that surprising when you consider my roots.

My mama was a wonderfully kind, loving person and she did all she could to keep my brother Peter and me believing in Santa for as long as possible. My earliest memories are of making construction paper chains and popcorn strings to make decorations for our Christmas tree. We hung anything we could find that was colorful and put those chains all around them. We didn't have lights, and Mama resisted our pleas to put real candles on the tree.

She would buy fruit and we would hang apples, oranges, and tangerines (my favorite). We would watch the fruit carefully so that if one began to look overripe, we would take it off the tree and eat it.

We always had a natural tree that was cut off our own,

or an unsuspecting neighbor's, property. My brother Robert, seven years older than me, was in charge of fetching the tree. He always chose a cedar variety. I loved the smell of that cedar in the house, and we kept it up so long that sometimes it looked like the pine beetle had its way with it before we finally took down the scrawny skeleton.

Mama never knew exactly where the tree came from, but Peter and I knew every tree and bush on our seven acres—and most of the ones on our neighbors' property. We never told Mama where we got the tree, because she would have had a fit if she knew they had been purloined in the pursuit of holiday cheer.

It was not until I was about ten that Robert finally let me go along on the hunt for the perfect tree. He had his eye on a grand specimen that was growing beside a pond on the Causey family farm, over a mile from our house. We took an axe and a bow saw, and made our way through the woods to the spot. The tree was located about halfway between the wood line and the pond and sat in an open clearing. It was at least twelve feet tall. We only wanted the top eight feet, so Robert outlined the plan to me as we stood in the shadow of the trees.

He would run out to the tree with the axe and chop the thing down. As soon as it toppled over, my job was to run out with the bow saw and cut it off at the designated spot. He would drop the axe, grab the tree, and run for the woods. I would pick up the axe and the saw and hightail it for the woods myself. There was only one complication. Mr. Causey had a reputation for protecting his property with a rifle!

At the given signal, Robert ran to the tree and began the chopping. At the third lick, the shooting began. We had agreed that we didn't think Causey would intend to shoot us, and we were well over a hundred yards away from his house. But I was concerned that in trying to miss us, he could do more damage.

At the sound of the first shot, Robert began chopping frantically. In a moment, over she went. I dashed out with the bow saw and was whipping that thing back and forth so fast I thought it would turn red hot. Robert's frenzied yelling for me to hurry up didn't help my nerves any more than the fusillade of gunfire.

The moment the trunk was severed, Robert snatched it up and dashed for the wood line. I picked up the axe and was right behind him. We ran on into the woods a good distance before the sound of rifle fire stopped. On the way home we figured that Causey would be in our backyard waiting for us, so we made our way carefully to determine if the coast was clear before delivering our bounty.

It was. We strolled casually into the yard after we had put the tools in the barn and nailed the crossbar stand to the bottom of the tree. We placed the tree in the customary spot in the living room as Mama made her usual exclamations of pleasure. We never did hear a word from Causey, and we never again crossed his property line for any reason.

As an aside, I later spent twenty years in the Marine Corps as an infantry officer. I still believe I was shot at more times that day on Causey's property than during all those years of being a professional target.

Our mama never threatened us with retribution from Santa if we didn't behave. She believed so strongly in the innate human quality of love, and the power of God's love, that she just wanted us to feel it and never wanted to take credit for it. Santa was a way she could show God's love to us through an anonymous third party.

Peter and I still talk about the night we actually saw Santa Claus. Mama always insisted we go to bed early on Christmas Eve, and we always fought sleep for several hours before we would drift off. But this one night was almost balmy, and we decided we would climb out the window of our room onto the front porch roof and wait to see Santa make his appearance.

We took our blankets along and wrapped ourselves in them. It was a breathlessly beautiful night with clear skies, millions of stars, and a near-full moon. It was just like a night earlier that year when we had sat out there to watch the Perseid meteor shower. That had been October 9, Peter's birthday, and it was one spectacular sight.

This evening, there was a hush over the land. This far out in the country, there was no ambient noise at all. We talked in whispers. We heard the Pringles' horse whinny in the barn across the fields. Then, suddenly, we nearly jumped out of our skins. There was the faint sound of sleigh bells somewhere in the distance. It could have been a mile, maybe even two miles away but it was the sound of sleigh bells for sure. Then we thought we saw an object moving through the sky. Slowly, magically, it moved directly across the face of the bright near-full moon! It looked like . . . it could only be . . . it had to be! It couldn't be anything or anyone else!

We grabbed our blankets, scrambled through the window into our room, and slid down the sash, locking it tight. We jumped into bed, covered up our heads and huddled together, not knowing whether we were scared to death or excited with anticipation. In moments, we were asleep.

Neither of us can remember the gifts we received the next morning, but we will both go to our graves convinced that on that magical, star-filled night, we saw the man!

That does not mean that there weren't some times our faith was called into question. Like late on Christmas Eve the year that I was ten. We had been shopping all day, and Peter and I had been sent on several meaningless errands so Mama and Daddy could make their secret purchases.

Peter and I went along with it since we knew we were to be the beneficiaries of this subterfuge. Daddy made several treks to the car with packages, and we were dying to look into those mysterious bundles, but knew better than to let on that we even knew about them, much less cared what was inside.

If I knew anything back then, it was the feeling of the back seat of our old '37 Chevrolet. I had sat in every conceivable position on it, and I had laid down to sleep there many times during the bumpy six-mile ride down the dirt road to our house. This night, it felt different. There seemed to be a new bump in the seat.

I slid my hand between the seat and the back and discovered a box under there. It felt about three inches thick, ten inches wide, and longer than I could reach in one direction. I found an open edge and eased my hand inside the box. I immediately recognized the shape and feel. It was the bolt handle of a rifle! Now that was exciting! I didn't think the rifle was for me, at my tender age, so I figured it must be for Robert.

The next morning as we were unwrapping gifts, I kept

watching for the long box. Finally, when all the gifts had been unwrapped, Mama told Robert to check behind the tree in the corner to see if there was anything left. Sure enough (surprise, surprise!) he pulled out a .22 caliber, single-shot rifle.

He very quickly became an expert shot and earned a reputation as a one-shot hunter. A bigger surprise was that Mama proved to be a better shooter than her son. One of her favorite tricks was to lay a Coke bottle on its side, then shoot through the neck of the bottle and blow out the bottom. She could also shoot well on the fly. We could toss a tin can into the air and she could hit it about every time. She could also shoot it straight from the hip.

But I digress. Back to Christmas!

Mama persisted in her commitment to keep Christmas and Santa alive for us. We always opened gifts on Christmas morning, never on Christmas Eve. Even when I came home from college, we continued the ritual. There were always some gifts from Santa that she had slipped under the tree after we had gone to bed. When I brought my own kids home years later, she always insisted that if they wanted to open gifts at her house, it had to be done on Christmas morning. My kids loved it as much as I did.

Maybe it was her persistence and her unwavering belief in the power of love that kept Christmas alive for me through all those years. And when I left the Marine Corps and stopped shaving, my beard grew out mostly white and helped the transition to the red suit. It was always down deep inside there somewhere. Just needed to be reenergized.

I promised I'd talk some more about the family of little people who play the role of elves at Stone Mountain Park. I want you to know what an incredible group of people they really are.

Pete is the patriarch. He comes from a family of eleven children, and he is the only little person in the bunch. His folks were farmers in Tifton, Georgia and he learned early to work hard at whatever job he undertook. He withstood a lot of ribbing and kidding from his family and friends in school, and rather than becoming embittered and angry about being "different," he developed a wonderful sense of humor. It's clear Pete is quite comfortable with the person he is.

Pete has been my most frequent elf, and we have become very close. He is a year older than me and we relate well to each other. We keep a running commentary about the visitors and the kids' requests all evening long. Pete has a warm, loving spirit about him.

Several years ago, Pete got laid off after a company merger and found himself idle for the first time in almost thirty years. His wife, Mary Alice, asked if I had any job openings at FODAC for him. I didn't have one, but I made one. Pete is now the first person anyone sees when they come to our building. He is the receptionist, customer service representative, and telephone operator, and he does a wonderful job of keeping all those responsibilities straight. He is extremely organized and completely un-flappable—the perfect person for the position.

Like many little people, Pete has some orthopedic problems and has had surgery on his hips and back. Fortunately, neither of his jobs requires him to be nim-ble and quick. His sweet disposition keeps him popular with the Santa visitors and the folks who come to FO-DAC for help.

Mary Alice is the matriarch—and, according to Pete, the boss—of the family. She was also raised in a loving, fun-filled family in DeKalb County, Georgia. Even as a child she wanted to be a teacher. For the past 31 years, she has realized that dream as a kindergarten teacher in the Henry County school system. Any time she is "elfing" at the park, someone will recognize her and greet her like a long lost relative. I guess in a sense, she is a relative to the many people whose lives she's touched.

Her favorite thing about elfing is the adoring, completely trusting look most kids bring to the throne. It is a look she sees often herself, I would think, but she says there is something different about seeing it in the Santa setting.

Sometimes her two worlds run together. Occasionally a kid from her classes will come to see Santa while she is the elf. Sometimes questions arise later. One day at school, a little boy demanded to know what was going on. She told him that she was also a teacher at the North Pole. He was freaked out that even the elves have to go to school. She assured him that people are going to school of some sort most of their lives to learn new things about their jobs or even to change professions. He didn't like that idea one bit!

Mary Alice did find out that the power of Santa works,

even when the big guy is not around. One year, she and her son Trent went to the Atlanta Farmer's Market to shop for a Christmas tree. Leaning out of the car, she asked one vendor if he had a special price for Santa and his elves. He laughed and said, "Sure, if he comes to get it himself."

Mary Alice said, "He couldn't come himself, but he sent us." Then she and Trent hopped out of the car.

The guy was completely taken aback when he saw them and said, "Well, I guess I do have a special price for y'all!" He marked down their chosen tree by fifty percent.

Mary Alice used that at school sometimes. She would tell boisterous kids that she knew Santa. Then one day, one of her students actually saw her with me at the park. She told him, "I told you I knew Santa, didn't I?" By the time school started the next day, every kid in the class knew that Mrs. Johnston was a personal friend of Santa Claus!

Heidi was the very first Johnston family elf I met, on the very first evening I arrived at Stone Mountain Park in 1991. I had been told there would be some little people there portraying elves, but in the excitement of that day, I had completely forgotten.

When I walked through the crowd outside the train station and went into the chicken restaurant where I would be working, there was Heidi. I was just greeting her when Trent walked up. I was meeting these folks for the first time, but the crowd watching would assume that I knew them very well. We agreed that we would get to know each other as the evening wore on.

Heidi was 18 and a senior in high school. Trent was 15 and a sophomore. I was immediately impressed by the wonderful personalities and delightful sense of humor these two had. They seemed very mature for their ages. In fact, they had been elfing longer than I had been Clausing, and I learned a lot from them on that first shift—and much more over the years. It was my distinct pleasure to watch these two grow up.

Heidi went away to college and became a nurse. One year she brought a handsome young man by to help her elf. She introduced him as Barry, her boyfriend. A year later, she returned with something sparkly on her hand.

She and Barry were engaged! He had passed his CPA exam, and wedding plans were well underway. I reminded her that I am an ordained minister. And before the evening was over, I had it all planned. We would have the wedding party and all the guests in their elfing outfits if appropriate; Santa in his red suit. It would be tons of fun—and the media would love it. The following Christmas, Heidi showed me her left hand again, and there was a wedding band to complement the diamond. Rats! She had gone ahead without me. But I was thrilled for the two of them and very excited about their future.

The next year, I heard that Heidi was pregnant, and soon another granddaughter was born into the Johnston family. This little girl was going to be a regular-sized person. Her name was Carrigan, and she was fortunate to inherit her parents' beauty genes. As is the nature of things, she would be taller than her parents by age nine. Heidi's mothering and work duties eventually led her away from elfing, but she remains a favorite of mine.

Trent grew up, too. During my second year at the

park, he decided he didn't want to go to college. He had already proven to me that he was an intelligent, energetic, industrious young man, and I knew he would do well in anything he attempted. The most impressive thing he has done is to create a remarkable family. He met Amber at a national meeting of the Little People of America in Chicago when they were both eighteen. They knew immediately that they wanted to be together forever, but waited until they were twenty to get married.

I met Amber at a Little People of America convention in Atlanta in 1997. She is a tiny lady with a huge heart. It was quite a sight to see her five years later when she was eight months pregnant. She looked like a basketball with legs, arms, and a head. She delivered a beautiful little guy they named Jonah. A couple of years later, his sister Elizabeth joined the family. She would be a little person, too. The doctor recommended that there be no more babies because Amber was so small, but that did not mean they couldn't add to their family. A year later, Trent and Amber heard about a girl in an orphanage—a little person. Life looked grim for her in Russia, as it was very unlikely that she would ever be adopted. Trent and Amber decided immediately that they would be her new parents.

Bureaucratic red tape threw delay after delay at them, but they were determined that they would not go home without this child. One week stretched into three. The girl's age put her right in between Jonah and Elizabeth, and she looked like she could be a blood sibling to them. Trent and Amber were determined to make her a part of their family. The officials finally relented and let them go home together. It took Anna about two minutes to fit into the family, and with three kids under four years old, life was fun for all.

Like many young children, they were all terrified of Santa. The fact that their "Poppi," Pete, was an elf for Santa did not impress them. They were not coming anywhere near me. It would take a dramatic lesson in 2005, during the FODAC Breakfast-with-Santa fundraiser, to get them past that.

The breakfast is held annually at the Marriott Evergreen Conference Center and Resort at Stone Mountain Park. Every year, it has grown in size and financial impact for FODAC. Pete and his family have always been elves at the event. That year, they decided it was time for Jonah to become an official elf. Amber fixed him an elf outfit, and he was very excited to be a real helper for Santa. And help he did. He was a bit shy at first, but soon he was dashing around among the presents, picking out special ones for each kid that came to my lap. Soon it was his turn to climb onto my lap, which he did without a moment's hesitation.

After that morning, he went home and told his sisters about it. A few days later, when they came to the park, they were all over me, too. They were all elves at the 2006 breakfast, and what a wonderful sight that was. And there was a new member of the family that year. Trent and Amber had heard about a baby in a Korean orphanage that was a little person and, with a lot less bureaucratic wrangling, Alex joined the family. Amber has proven to be a wonderful mother, and Mary Alice is an apt mentor for her. It is such a wonderful thing to watch the whole family interacting with these active, energetic kids.

Throw in Heidi's Carrigan and Bunny's full-sized

daughter Halle, and the whole house fills up very quickly with love and laughter. Sitting and watching, one would wonder why all families can't be like this, simply loving one another.

Trent has a few fond memories of elfing. One is the time he noticed that the little girl on my lap had her shoes on the opposite feet. He pointed that out to me, and I said to her, "You have your shoes on the wrong feet, Sweetie."

She looked down a moment, then looked back up with a frown. She said, "These are the only feet that I have!"

But one of Trent's favorite stories is the night a young couple came to sit on my lap. As I always do, I asked if they were dating. They said yes, so I told them to hold hands for the photo. After as it was taken, the young man continued to hold his girl's hand. He said, "I have chosen this time and this place to ask this question."

Trent and I both heard that and knew something was about to happen. Trent jumped off his stool beside me and ran around in front so he could see their faces.

The man pulled his arm from behind me and with an obviously practiced move, popped open a little black box. "I love you with all my heart," he said. "Will you marry me?"

Wow, I thought. A proposal, right here on my lap! How neat!

He had caught his girlfriend completely off guard. She gave a long pause, then looked again at the ring and blurted out, "What, are you kidding me? No way! Never! Forget it!" She jumped off my lap and nearly knocked Trent over on her way to the door.

The guy just sat there in shock. In a moment I said, "Don't just sit here, boy. Go get her!" He jumped up and took off after her.

I don't know the rest of that story, but I did share it with another young couple who came to have their pictures taken on Santa's lap. The next Christmas they returned—and showed me their wedding rings. They had come back to the park that spring for the laser show, and at the height of the fireworks, he had asked her to marry him. She had, of course, said yes.

Pete and Mary Alice's daughter Bunny is another wonderful mother and dynamic person. She's also a great elf. I get the impression that nothing is going to stand in the way of this dynamo. She is a real go-getter. One night, during a lull in the action, she decided to go get a cup of hot chocolate. On her way back, she stepped up on the stage and tripped over the edge of a rug in front of the throne. She came crashing down on her belly, right in front of the throne. I shouted and jumped up to help her. But before I could lift a finger, she went crawling across the floor to retrieve her cup of hot chocolate (still safe under the lid), which had rolled away from her. She set it upright and then jumped up on her own. She picked up her cup, sat back down in her chair and brushed off my expressions of concern. "I fall all the time," she said, sipping her treasured drink.

Bunny likes to work the line some, too. I have seen her standing right up against a reluctant visitor, lecturing him and shaking her finger in his face, which she has to reach up to get to. Now she is a supervisor in an office, and I know I wouldn't want her upset with me!

Bunny's husband, Barry (yes, both Bunny and Heidi married men named Barry!), is a fun elf, too. He likes to work the line and try to get potential screamers used to the idea of seeing Santa before the moment arrives.

One night Walt and Sue Ellsmore, who worked for me at FODAC, brought their grandson, Austin, to see Santa. He didn't quite make it. He looked through the window and didn't cry, but he let them know he was not going to come inside the building to see me. Barry had volunteered at FODAC and knew Walt and Sue. He asked me what they were doing, standing outside. I told him that Austin didn't want to come in. He said, "Well, I can handle that." He went out and I watched as he put his arm around the kid (they were about the same size) and whispered in his ear. In a moment they came through the door, hand in hand. Austin got right up on my lap, and gave me his list while Walt took a whole bunch of pictures. I never did find out just what Barry had said to Austin, but whatever it was, it worked and had a lasting effect. Austin was never afraid of me again.

I mentioned the yearly elf gathering at the park, so let me tell you about the most recent one. They are always so special to me—and to the visitors who are lucky enough to see it. There are always a bunch of little people, elves and their children, all over the park. The Johnston family invites some of their friends to come, too. Last year, another couple came and brought their daughter. This little girl is not just a little person; she is a very little person. She is about five, but is only about the size of an eighteen-month-old. She is a beautiful child, but tiny. She ran to me like I was her grandpa and jumped up onto my stool, then my lap. She talked to me like she was a grown-up. She knew exactly what she wanted, including brand names and model numbers. She was such a delight, I didn't want her to get down. Lucky for me, she came back later to ask some more questions and supply some additional information about her Christmas list.

## BEING SANTA CLAUS

Playing Santa Claus has given me many moments of sheer joy. And by far the most fun and satisfaction have come when I was able to be Santa to kids and grown-ups alike.

For years I had heard preachers talk about how God has a plan for your life and how you have to work at finding what that plan and purpose are for you. I never could have dreamed that one day my purpose would become so completely clear to me.

In January of 1979, a young man with cerebral palsy began attending the church where I was a member. Over the next two years we had a nodding acquaintance. I knew his first name, but feeling like a coward, I tried to avoid direct eye contact with him. Looking him in the eyes would necessitate speaking, but what do you say to someone in a wheelchair? What do you say to a person whose body is twisted and racked with spasms? What in the world do you say?

Over the next couple of months, we began to sit and talk. I found that he was a bright, well-read man, and an interesting conversationalist. I became embarrassed that for so long I had avoided getting to know him. One Sunday in February of 1981, I visited him in his apartment. He lived in a complex near the church. It was called Columbia Place Apartments, and had been built for wheelchair users. I visited him often over the next few months, and one time I put a new light bulb in the light fixture over his bathroom sink.

I was shocked to discover that the simple process of replacing a light bulb gave me a feeling of accomplishment and satisfaction I had never experienced, even when I had won awards for marksmanship, sales, and writing. Those were individual accomplishments; there was something different about helping another person do something he couldn't do for himself.

On my next visit I changed a light bulb for another person in the same complex. Soon, I was changing light bulbs throughout Columbia Place, and then I started doing other small chores. My building skills were being put to use.

The more I did, the more that joyful feeling swept over me. It wasn't too long before I was going through the complex looking for ways to be helpful. I spent hours talking with people who had all kinds of disabilities, and began to learn about the problems they faced and how they dealt with them. I began to learn that people with physical limitations are just like everyone else. They have the same hopes and dreams we all do, and their disability may or may not impede their progress toward those goals.

I learned that some people completely collapse when struck by a disabling injury or illness. Others seem to be energized to overcome.

One of the biggest problems faced by wheelchair-dependent people is that of getting around. The simplest things, like shopping or running errands, can be a tremendous challenge. While on a sales call in Athens, Georgia, I drove by a Dodge dealership. On a whim, I pulled into the used car lot. I told the salesman I was looking for a van to transport folks in wheelchairs, and he took me to the back of the lot where a retired Head Start school bus was sitting. It was a faded yellow bus with black spray paint covering the lettering on the sides, front, and rear. It looked awful, but I was more interested in how it ran and what it cost.

The salesman took me back to the offices, where he talked privately with the used car sales manager. In a few minutes he came back and told me the bus was for sale for $1,200, but we could have it for $400. "Sold!" I said.

The church I was attending paid for a folding ramp and four wheelchair tie-downs in the bus, and I began hauling folks around. We went to shopping centers, restaurants, concerts, and special events. There were big changes going on in my life during these years. I was divorced, then I met and married Annie. But the involvement with the people with disabilities was a constant that I knew was evolving into something greater.

At that point, I was fully employed as a salesman of medical diagnostic equipment and supplies. I was covering Georgia and Alabama, as well as large portions of Tennessee and South Carolina. With all this ministry activity going on, I wasn't spending as much time on the road as needed, but in spite of that, my sales continued to climb. I began to have the feeling that someone up there was definitely looking out for me. I was beginning to sense God's powerful presence and His incredible peace within my soul.

A young lady named Ann Searcy started coming to our Monday night Bible study sessions. After she had attended for a while, she invited her uncle, Dan Barnes, and his wife Mary, to attend one night. They were delightful folks who seemed quite taken to be included in a room full of people with wheelchairs or other mobility aids. They asked a lot of questions after the session, and told us they were members of Mount Carmel Christian Church in Decatur. Mr. and Mrs. Barnes said they were going to speak to the senior minister about what we were doing.

I knew a little about Mount Carmel Christian Church. The baccalaureate services for three of my children's high school graduations had been held there. I had been impressed with the senior pastor, Jack Ballard, on those occasions. Jack had been the senior minister for over 30 years, and he had built the church into the largest congregation in that part of the county. Mount Carmel performed the Living Christmas Tree program each year, and we had taken our old bus loaded with disabled folks to enjoy it for the last five years. It was a wonderful, highly professional performance.

In a few days, Dan called to say that he had spoken to his Kiwanis Club of South DeKalb, and they wanted to give us $500. But there was a wrinkle. They couldn't just give the money to Ed and Annie; they had to give it to an organization. Annie and I spent a couple of weeks trying to decide on a name. We kept coming back to the fact that we were simply friends of several people with disabilities, all of whom were adults. We considered several alternatives and finally settled on calling our efforts Friends of Disabled Adults, Inc.—FODA for short.

We hired an attorney I knew to file the incorporation documents. The Kiwanis Club didn't wait for the paperwork; they sent the check as soon as we told them our name. We used that check to open the FODA checking account. We also called the IRS and had them send us the packet of papers to file for 501(c)(3) status and had the attorney draw up a set of bylaws for us. That process would take over a year, and several refilings, before we were granted permanent IRS nonprofit status. That document was dated November 10, 1987. Funny, I had celebrated that date as the birthday of the Marine Corps for over 20 years, and now it was a birthday of sorts for our new endeavor.

As we pondered all of this, we had a phone call from Jack Ballard, the senior minister of Mount Carmel. He had heard about our Bible study and the things we were doing from Dan and Mary Barnes and asked us to come to his office the following Monday. I have to admit it was exciting to wonder just what might come of our visit.

The meeting began with Jack telling us of all the ways Mount Carmel had been involved in ministering to people with disabilities over the years. Jack's own secretary was a polio survivor. He had visited her in the hospital right after she was diagnosed at age eighteen. He promised her a job then, and he kept his promise. And she would hold that job for thirty-eight years.

Jack had helped a man named Jim Pierson realize his dream of a home for people with mental disabilities where they would be treated with Christian love and given the opportunity to become all that they could be. Mount Carmel's Church Builders program built the facility in Tennessee where that dream was made real.

We told Jack about our work with the people we knew and invited him to visit the apartment complex where they lived. He said he would like to get Jim Pierson to come from Tennessee and go with him to get another perspective. When we left, he said he would call Jim and be in touch with us.

On the ride home, we calculated that it would be at least a couple of weeks before they'd be able to schedule a visit. But when we got home, there was a message on our answering machine from Jack. Jim would be in town on Thursday! Clearly Jack was a person who made things happen. We would soon learn just how true that was.

We met at Mount Carmel that Thursday, and all four of us went to the apartment complex in my company car. We toured the place and showed them all the little repair jobs I had done. Those two grown men stood in the middle of the courtyard and cried real tears as they saw the size of the need we had tried to fill. They understood the need for our undertaking even more than we did.

When we arrived back at Mount Carmel, Jack said, "I'm going to talk to our missions committee and see if we can't add you to our missions program and get you some financial support."

Annie and I couldn't help but wonder how much support it would be. We figured it would take a while to hold a committee meeting, bring it up, discuss it, and get a vote on it. We thought that some of the committee members would want to see our work for themselves.

We got home and, would you believe, there was another message from Jack. He had already gotten the approval from the missions committee to support us—starting on the next mission Sunday. The amount of that support would be $1,000 per month! I found out years later that the moment he got back to his office, he set up a conference call with all the members of the missions committee, made a presentation about our project, and called for a vote on supporting us. The vote was unanimous.

We collapsed on the sofa with tears of joy, shock,

thanksgiving, and every other possible emotion. We had been doing our thing for over five years and we had had a total of $400 worth of help, including the $250 in the as-yet-unmodified bus sitting in our driveway. Here was the money to make our ministry really viable. It was just a week before that we had bought the bus. And look what had happened already! To Annie it was a matter of fact—acknowledgment that God had kept His promise. To me it was an awesome lesson in trust, taught to me by my sweetie and a loving God. It was a lesson that was hammered into my hard head again and again before I reached the point that Annie had already achieved, where I could simply step out in faith knowing that God would honor that trust.

We also reconsidered those series of "coincidences" that had brought us to this point. There were just too many times that impossible things happened for there not to have been a power greater than ourselves working things out. Clearly that power had plans for us that were bigger than we were. The song, "Awesome God" became an anthem for us.

Those miracles continued, and soon it became apparent that God had a plan for us. I felt like I was barreling down a beautiful highway in a Rolls Royce without a steering wheel. I didn't know where we were headed, but I did know we were getting there in a style I couldn't even imagine.

Early on, I asked Jack what the process was for ordination in his church. He suggested that I attend Atlanta Christian College and learn more about the church and the fellowship it belonged to. I called the college, met with the dean of men, and was enrolled for the term starting in January 1987. I was still working full time, so I signed up for one evening class and two classes that met all day one Monday a month. I was required to call my regional manager every Monday at nine. Occasionally, he would ask me to meet him for lunch on that day. Classes began at 8 a.m., but my teacher agreed to let me out of class for the few minutes it took to make that call. My boss never once asked me to meet him on my class days, but he did ask me three times on the Mondays when I did not have class. My heart was stirred with the undeniable truth that someone else was taking care of my schedule. God Himself was directing my path.

It was an arduous undertaking, but I set my mind to it and pressed on. About a year later we decided that it was time to quit my overpaid job as a salesman and start helping folks full time.

Later that fall, Annie and I were having dinner in a Chinese restaurant when I noticed a woman staring blatantly at me. I had never been checked out so shamelessly in my life. I began to wonder what she was seeing, and I checked to make sure I was properly buttoned and zipped. When she and her friend finished their meal, they came to our table and asked me if I was a professional Santa Claus. I told her no, but that I would like to be. She handed me a card and told me to call her. This new venture would provide not only a wonderful element of fun and love in our lives, but would be a big help financially as well.

But—slow learner that I am—I still did not make a connection between the ministry and Santa. It wouldn't be until the middle of my first season as a mall Santa when I would realize that there was no coincidence about this converging of tasks.

Here's why. When we started, the one thing we were sure we wanted to do was provide transportation for folks. Four days after we started full-time, I had a call from one of our folks telling me there was a wheelchair by the dumpster at Columbia Place Apartments if I wanted it. I figured I could fix it up and give it to someone who needed it, so I went and got it. That simple act put us on the path of what would become the most important thing our ministry would accomplish. Over these next twenty years we would find, collect, refurbish, and give away over 17,000 wheelchairs—manuals of all kinds, electrics, and scooters. It didn't take long before newspapers began to call, and in 1992, NBC Nightly News ran a piece about what this Santa was doing in his real workshop. When he introduced the piece, Tom Brokaw referred to me as "the real thing." From then on I was known as the "Wheelchair Santa."

We started out providing services to adults. But it soon became apparent that God was sending us children who needed help. When I was looking for parts for the first five wheelchairs, I connected with a small company in Tucker owned by a delightful couple named Joe and Kathy Mc-Gehee. They must have thought I was crazy when I told them what we intended to do. But they did get the parts for me—and sold them to us at a better-than-retail price. A few months later, Kathy called me and told me they had twenty-four children's wheelchairs that they would give us. We had never intended to do children's chairs, but this was an offer I couldn't refuse. I told Kathy we would take the chairs, and when I hung up the phone I said out loud, "I guess the Lord wants us to do chairs for children."

One of the first to call us after we got the chairs was the family of a four-year-old named Kimberly. She had suffered a stroke and had lost her ability to speak and to walk. She simply could not sit still. The family had cleared their living room and furnished it with mattresses. Kimberly's parents had a cheesecake business in the basement of their house, and one of them had to be upstairs to watch Kimberly all the time. They were hoping that a wheelchair she could be strapped into would enable her to sit still at least part of the time.

They brought Kimberly to my house for an assessment. She was a beautiful little lady, but her spasms were awful. I was not at all sure whether a wheelchair would help control her involuntary movements. I picked out a chair, cleaned it up, set up the positioning pads and straps, and called Kimberly back. I placed her in the chair and fastened the seatbelt. She was still having spasms. I put a butterfly brace across her chest, and her legs and arms continued to flail. I put the knee separator in place, pulled her feet into position on the footrests, and strapped them down.

Kimberly took a deep breath, raised her head up to look at the TV on the shelf over the workbench, gave a long sigh, put her hands in her lap, and sat perfectly still. Her mom and dad grabbed each other and started to cry. Between sobs, her mother said, "That is the first time she's sat still while awake in over a year."

Nobody was more surprised than I was. I said out loud, "Thank you, Lord."

Mom responded, "Yes, praise the Lord. And thank you too, Santa."

Kimberly improved over the years and was able to attend public school. I lost track of her in more recent years, but my hope is that her life has been filled with calm and quiet moments.

A special group of ladies made this next Santa encounter so very special. Kim was with the Fraternal Order of Eagles Ladies Auxiliary in Doraville, Georgia. The group was raising money to buy a wheelchair for a little guy named Jacob. He was only eight years old and had severe cerebral palsy. He had two wishes: to get an electric wheelchair and to go to Disney World. His therapists had agreed that Jacob's spasms would keep him from being able to operate an electric wheelchair. But his parents felt he was more coordinated than that. The fraternal group had decided to raise the money, get the chair, and see how Jacob handled it.

They were making some progress toward their goal of $6,400 when Kim called FODAC to see if we would make a donation to their wheelchair fund. When she learned that we would GIVE him a wheelchair, Kim couldn't believe it!

We had a virtually new chair that had been sitting for

a few months, waiting for the right person. It was the perfect size for Jacob. His parents brought Jacob in for his
first fitting, and he was enthralled by the special room
for kids we call Santa's office. When the door opens, all
kinds of things begin to happen. The lights on the Christmas tree and around the room come on. Several animated characters begin to move. Christmas music plays and
an animated Santa sings out, "A Holly Jolly Christmas."
Two electric trains begin to chug—one around a track just
above the door and the other at the base of the tree. My
gold throne spends most of the year there. A huge, stuffed
Mickey Mouse keeps it warm.

We decided to have Santa there to make the delivery. As it just so happened, this was the ten-thousandth
wheelchair we gave away. I made sure I was there when
it happened.

Jacob brought an entourage with him. His mom and
dad, his grandmother, and several of the Eagles ladies
came to see Jacob receive his new chair. We also had two
television crews there to record the event. It was quite a
moment. Within a few minutes, after brief instructions

from Bruce Williams, our volunteer electric shop manager and wheelchair user himself, Jacob took the controls and drove himself across the room. The crowd burst into applause. This was the very first time Jacob had controlled his own movements anywhere. There were no dry eyes in the place. Even Vernon Jones, the DeKalb County CEO, had tears on his cheeks. Bruce asked Jacob if he liked the chair, and Jacob nodded. Then Bruce asked if he was happy. And Jacob whispered, "Yes."

After a hug from Santa, Jacob was anxious to get outside and get on with the rest of his life, so we stood in the lobby and watched him go. His mother came to me and threw her arms around my neck, then worked her way down the chain of command, hugging everybody in sight. She finally managed to squeak out a "thank you" as she followed her son out the door.

We still saw Jacob, as he would stop in occasionally to thank us again. At the next year's Walk and Roll fundraiser, he won the prize for raising the most money of all the several hundred attendees. His just being there driving his wheelchair was the best part. It was a brand new chair, paid for by his dad's insurance plan. Once the therapists saw that he could handle driving the electric chair from FODAC, they approved his request for one. He was riding in high style now, and he used the chair FODAC gave him when he was at school.

------------------------------------ RACHEL ------------------------------------

One of our most defining and joyful Santa moments came with a child we would never actually meet.

I was sitting at my desk at FODAC when a call came in from a soldier at Fort Riley, Kansas. His name was George and he was helping a local group raise money for a wheelchair for a three-year-old named Rachel. She had cerebral palsy, but it had affected only her legs. She could not support her weight or walk, but the rest of her body was fine. Her father was a farmer and, like many small farmers, times were tough. It looked like they were about to lose their farm. They could not afford health insurance.

George had helped out at a barbecue dinner the previous Saturday. It was a cold, rainy day, and they had managed to raise only $400 toward their goal of $7,000.

George was telling me all this as a preamble to asking us for money for a chair for Rachel. I interrupted to tell him that we didn't have any money we could contribute, but that we could give Rachel an electric wheelchair, custom fitted for her. He stammered for a moment, then asked, "Do you really mean that?"

I told him that all I needed for him to do was send me some photos of Rachel sitting in a kitchen chair so I could set up the wheelchair properly, and I would find a way to get it to them absolutely free of any charges. He said he could do that—but it took some more convincing to get him to believe that it would actually happen.

As soon as I hung up the phone, I went out into the warehouse and found a very nice Invacare Jaguar. The red paint on it was in great shape. It barely looked used, although the rear tires were both flat. I pushed it into the shop and told the guys to get it ready. It was going to Kansas.

On the same day that Rachel's pictures arrived, the shop guys brought me the chair. It looked terrific—cleaned, polished, and with solid inserts in the tires so they would never go flat again. I adjusted the footrests according to the photos. I sat on the armrests and gave it the torture test. I even drove it around for awhile myself. It worked perfectly.

Bob McMullen, one of our volunteers, took a donated pallet and cut it in half. He strapped the chair onto it, used some donated plywood to build a crate around it, packed the crate with donated stuffed animals, nailed the top on, painted "to Rachel, from Santa" on the side of the crate, and pronounced it ready to go.

Gene Seay, one of our friends at Mount Carmel Christian Church, arranged for the chair to get a free ride to George at Fort Riley. I took our donated forklift and loaded the crate into the back of a donated pickup truck, then drove it over to the freight company near the airport. The gas had been purchased using money we had gotten for aluminum cans collected and recycled by another Mount Carmel friend and volunteer.

Four days later I got a call from George. He started off the conversation by saying, "I know why you do what you do."

"You do?"

"Yeah, I do. The feeling that I got from delivering that chair to Rachel last night has to be happening at your place all the time. You do that because of the good feeling you get every time that happens."

I told him, "Yeah, that is a good feeling. But a better one is when I know that the Lord put this deal together, working out the details way ahead of when they were needed, and that he covered every detail of the costs."

He told me that when they opened the crate, Rachel squealed with delight at the sight of the stuffed animals. And then, when Rachel sat in the chair and put her hands on the controls, the squeals really got going. It was dark, so they went inside and Rachel went driving around, crashing into the furniture and walls, squealing all the way. Her parents, George, and the friends he had taken over there with him were all squealing, too!

I told him that the wheelchair had been sent to us by a woman in Appleton, Wisconsin, who had been collecting used equipment for a while when she saw a story about us on television and decided we should have it. A Kimberly-Clark Corporation truck driver had brought the stuff (free of charge) to Atlanta on one of his trips to the local office. Total expenditures for this entire venture? Zero. Nothing.

Nada. Not a penny. We do serve an awesome God.

A few days later I got a call from Rachel's mother. She told me she had not been able to call earlier because she was too emotional. She told me that the morning after the chair arrived, she and Rachel went out into the yard. Rachel was driving around, still squealing, when she pulled up next to the steps where Mom was sitting.

Her eyes were all big and she was so excited. "Mom!" she exclaimed. "Mom, I can feel the wind in my ears!"

Mom and I had to pause for a moment to let the lumps clear from our throats. She went on, "My little girl can't run and play like the other kids, so she never felt the wind before. For the first time in her life, she could feel the wind because of something she was doing herself, operating her wheelchair. I just want to thank you for putting the wind in my little girl's ears."

Now I really had a lump! I couldn't respond.

Mom went on, "We saved the side of the crate that says, 'to Rachel, from Santa,' and we are all going to be believers for the rest of our lives."

I managed to recover enough to thank her for the call

and to tell her it would be one I would remember forever.

Several months later, I had a letter from Rachel's Mom. She told me that they had lost the farm and had moved to town where her husband had taken an industrial job. They lived on Main Street. Every day Rachel rode up to the businesses along the street and visited the many friends she had made. She had become a "real gadabout," where before she had been very shy and withdrawn. Mom sent me a picture of Rachel sitting in the chair and looking toward the camera. Her beautiful face had an impish grin and was framed by a mantle of bright red curls. What a delightful picture.

George was right. That is why I do what I do—that good feeling.

Sometimes that good feeling has nothing to do with children. Relating Santa's love and God's love to these special people required some extra effort, with sometimes surprising rewards.

I had seen Anne Crooke occasionally around Columbia Place. Usually, she was going to get her mail. She always wore a Vanity Fair nightgown or pajamas with a Vanity Fair robe. I knew what apartment she lived in, but she had remained aloof from us and we left her alone. We exchanged pleasant greetings, but she didn't seem to want conversation. She refused offers to join our Bible study group or to participate in any of the events we set up. From the others, I discovered that she was a chain smoker and had a drinking problem.

Don Nelson was a friend of hers and did small chores for her like walking her dog and going to the store. Then one day, Don told me that Anne wanted me to take her to the dentist.

When I arrived for the trip, she was wearing her usual night gown and robe. It soon became clear that she didn't have any regular clothes to wear. Her dentist was near Piedmont Hospital in Atlanta. Over the years I took her there, and also to her doctor, many times. I got to know both of them rather well.

At one point she told me that her sister had died, and that she was unable to get to North Carolina for the funeral. Later she said that her sister had left her an inheritance of over $30,000. She had a woman whom she called her "maid," who would come in once a week or so and clean her apartment and go grocery shopping for her. I discovered that most of the "groceries" were in liquid form. Somehow I just knew there was something fishy about that arrangement.

Then, disaster struck. Don Nelson was walking his and Anne's dogs on the sidewalk along Columbia Drive, a very busy street. The dogs were playing and nipping at each other and Anne's dog, Poochie, jumped into the street. He was instantly hit by a passing car. Don carried the body back to Anne's apartment and laid it on her table. Anne, understandably, wept and wailed, and Don finally had to pry the body from her arms to take it out for burial. She continued her demonstrative mourning. She got her bottles out and proceeded to get completely inebriated. Her maid found her in that condition the next day, and doing as she was told, went and bought more booze.

Anne told everyone that she was going to drink herself to death, and she worked hard at it. She did not leave her bed for the next two weeks, not even for a trip to the bathroom. I did not go by her apartment during that time, but I did hear from Don that it was getting really awful in there. One day the woman who ran the Meals on Wheels program called me, saying that her delivery volunteers reported that Anne was in real trouble. She did not appear to be eating the meals they were delivering, and she was completely drunk every day. A little later, Don's dad, Dick Nelson, called and told me we were going to have to do something. I had a transport to do, but said I would come over there when it was done. I asked if he and Don could get her cleaned up. He promised to try. When I called,

Dick told me Anne was refusing to let them wash her. I spoke to Anne and told her that I was coming over, and that she'd better be cleaned up when I got there. I was not going to take no for an answer.

I arrived at Columbia Place as soon as possible. Several people were there, and Anne was sitting on her somewhat cleaner but still uninhabitable bed. It was awful. The several layers of blankets, sheets, and waterproof pads did not make it any better. I sat in a chair across from her, observing her completely drunken state. I said quietly, "Hey, Anne, what is going on?"

She answered in a near stupor, "My Poochie got killed and I am going to drink myself to death."

"Well, I really don't want you to do that," I answered. "Why don't we see what your doctor has to say about it?"

"I don't care what he says," she mumbled. "I got no reason to live anymore. I just want to die."

As she was talking, I was dialing her doctor's number. To my profound shock, I reached him. After identifying myself, he said, "Well, hi, Ed. How is Ms. Crooke doing?" I told him about the dog, and that she was drunk and intended to do herself in. He said we couldn't let that happen but that he couldn't admit her for being drunk. I looked down at her feet hanging off the side of the bed and told him that her circulation problem was worse than ever and that she needed treatment soon.

He said, "Great, then she definitely needs to be in the hospital for at least three weeks. We can work together to get her in a safer place."

I told him I was bringing her to Piedmont, and he agreed to meet us in the ER. I hung up and called an ambulance service. I wasn't about to transport her in my van. I didn't think she could sit up in a wheelchair, and I didn't have a gurney. Of course Anne had heard this conversation and was hollering that she was not going to go to "any stupid hospital," and she didn't care what I said. The other people in the room watched quietly as the drama unfolded.

While we waited for the ambulance I took all her booze to the sink and personally poured every drop down the drain. Everyone watched. Some offered to help, but that was one job I wanted to do myself, giving her reason to be mad at me only. Next, I went through her dresser drawers and collected her bank statement, checks, and checkbook, along with other personal records.

When the ambulance came, they brought in a gurney and I motioned to Anne and said, "Take her to Piedmont ER." An EMT asked if we were related. I told her, "I am embarrassed to tell you this, but she's my mama." (Yes, it was a lie, which was later confessed and forgiven.)

Anne exploded in protestations, "I am not his mama. I don't even know him. I don't even have any children. Don't let him do this to me. I don't want to go to the hospital. Don't you dare take me to the hospital!"

Looking at the EMTs, shaking my head, I said, "She does this to me all the time. I am so embarrassed." They nodded. Then they forced her onto the gurney and strapped her down. She went out the door, hollering all the way.

I told the people there to take her mattress and bedding out to the dumpster and to take the bed (a lovely antique spool bed) outside and hose it off. They soaked the floor under the bed with disinfectant soap.

I got to the hospital before the ambulance and went straight to the ER to talk to the doctor. When the ambulance pulled up, the crew told me she had hollered so much that she'd hyperventilated. They'd had to give her oxygen during the ride. And they were glad to get rid of her.

The doctor took Anne back into an exam room, and I went home. A few days later I called and talked to the nurses on her floor. They begged me to come and get her out of there. I could hear her yelling over the phone. I told the nurse I would come down in a few days. The doctor had promised me three weeks of hospitalization, and I was going to use all of it. During that time I cleaned out Anne's apartment and stored her furniture at FODAC. I cancelled her phone and stopped her month-to-month lease. I talked to a social worker at the hospital, asking her to find a rehabilitation/nursing home that would take Anne in directly from the hospital. Medicare would pay for a certain number of days, and I knew she needed every one of them.

I went to the hospital at the end of her second week.

When I walked into her room, she looked completely different. She was stone sober and her eyes were clear. Unfortunately, her temperament had not changed. She lit into me like a mad hornet. She yelled and hollered, threatening me with several manners of revenge. She told me she was going to go back to her apartment and take up right where she left off. I announced that she no longer had an apartment and that she was going into a nursing home. Now she really went berserk, with more screams, threats, and ugly words. The one thing she did not do was get violent. I smiled at her once and said, "One day you are going to thank me for this." She did not calm down, so I just left.

During this time I went through her bank statements and cancelled checks. I also found a few grocery store receipts. I matched up the transaction dates and discovered that her "maid" had been paying for $50 to $60 worth of groceries with checks of $250 to $300. She had no doubt pocketed the difference. She had even written herself a couple of checks for $500 and signed Anne's name. I wrote all this out on a lined pad. Anne's $30,000 inheritance had decreased by $18,000 in five months.

The social worker called and told me she had placed Anne in a nursing home near DeKalb Medical Center. Anne was transferred by ambulance, and I was in the business office when she arrived. Once again, I told them I was her son. I could hear her bellyaching when they came in the back door. I went out the front. I was going to let her stew in her own juices for another week or so more.

I called a man I knew who owned a personal care home in Tucker. He told me that he could manage to take Anne for the $1700 monthly income she had, although the normal rate was much more.

I went to the nursing home and the moment I walked in the room, Anne took off again with the crabbing and grousing. "Get me out of here," she screamed. Pointing at her three roommates, she said, "That woman is crazy and just talks gibberish all the time, that one just sits and stares at me, and the other one cries all the time. I can't take any more of this place."

I ignored her demonstration and sat down on the bed beside her. I showed her the lined pad and explained how her maid had been ripping her off and keeping her drunk so she could steal from her. I documented every entry, and proved that she could have no doubt that what I had found was true. I told her that this amounted to felony theft. I asked her if she wanted to prosecute her maid. She pondered that for a while and then said, "No." I said that I was going to call her maid and tell her what we found, and that if she ever showed up anywhere near Anne I would have her arrested and prosecuted.

Of course, the maid denied everything, but said she would not come back.

I went back to the nursing home a few days later, and Anne had calmed down some. This time she quietly begged me to get her out of there. I told her about the personal care home in Tucker. She said she didn't know where Tucker was and didn't want to move so far away. But I did my best to explain that this would be good for her.

Annie went to a thrift store and bought five outfits for her. We had them cleaned and put on hangers. I went back to the nursing home and showed Anne the outfits, one at a time. She found something wrong with every one of them, until the last one. She said, "I guess I could wear that one." I told her I would get a nurse to help her get ready, but she just whipped off her top and said, "Here, throw it over me." I did, in a big hurry.

She protested all the way out to Tucker. But when we pulled into the parking lot and she saw the building, her entire tone changed.

"This is very nice," she whispered. I rolled her up to the door and as we went in, she exclaimed in as sweet a voice as you could imagine, "Hello, everybody. My name is Anne. How are you?"

The manager had been expecting us, and took us to see the room and other amenities. I told Anne that I was prepared to move her furniture into her room, and that I had ordered her a nice custom-made mattress for her bed. I spoke about it as if it was a done deal. She went along with it.

A few of us moved her furniture into the room and hung her pictures on the walls. I told Marilyn, the manager, that if she or anyone else got booze for Anne I would have them fired. She knew I could do that, and made sure her staff understood it, too.

Anne was very happy at that place, and to spice it up some, Annie and I took her out to eat once a week or so. She always loved those times. We took her to Mount Carmel Church some, too. That was another special treat.

Two years went by. One night during dinner, she suddenly said, "I hate to admit it, but you were right. I am glad you took me out of Columbia Place. I am sure I would be dead by now and would have missed out on all this fun and the wonderful life I have now."

I just said, "You're welcome."

In time, the home was sold to new owners. I talked to them, and they agreed to keep Anne on for $1700 for as long as they could. But in a couple more years they told her they had to raise the rent. So Annie and I went looking for a new home for Anne. A staff member at Tucker also worked in another residence, and we went to see it. It was very nice, and in a week, Anne was moved in. The owner of this new abode took Anne lots of places, and occasionally brought her to Mount Carmel. One Sunday night I was sitting in my regular seat at the end of a pew when I felt movement to my left. I turned and there was Anne. I jumped, feigning being frightened. I said, "Good grief, woman. That's enough to scare a man to death, sneaking up on him like that. That was a mean, rotten thing to do."

She leaned over to me and said, "Is that any way to talk to your mama?" I just about fell out of my seat. That was the first and last reference she ever made about my outrageous story all those years ago.

Anne loved hearing about all the good things going on at FODAC and all the people we were helping. She delighted in my Santa role, and I always made a couple of appearances at her personal care home. She loved it and behaved like she was my mama. She gave me a precious Santa figurine, which I keep by my bed even now.

Anne developed emphysema from all those years of smoking, and her systems slowly shut down. She died in November of 2001, while my Santa season was in full swing. She had lived nine years since I took her screaming and kicking out of Columbia Place. I led her memorial service one evening at her personal care home, and several of her friends were there.

There was one sad line in her obituary. "There were no survivors."

Over the course of these twenty years, we have met many other remarkable people among the 60,000 or so who have come to us for help. It has been a constant source of amazement how some people collapse completely at the slightest interruption in their mobility, and yet others can take almost anything in stride and keep on going.

----------- JOHN HOWARD HAIRE, JR. -----------

John Howard Haire, Jr., was the son of a former mayor pro tem of the city of Atlanta. John grew up as a person of privilege, an only child, doted on by his mother and father. As our nation's involvement in World War II loomed, John wanted to be a pilot. He enrolled in the V12 program at the University of Georgia as soon as it was established. He became a multi-engine instructor pilot and flew all the multi-engine aircraft in the U.S. inventory.

His marriage to a society debutante made all the papers. When I saw pictures years later, I saw that he was an incredibly handsome figure in his uniform. His gorgeous bride was from a prominent Atlanta family.

John was discharged at the end of the war and just a few weeks later suffered a massive cerebral hemorrhage. His mother moved into his room at the VA hospital and catered to his every need. It was clear that John's life had changed forever. He could not talk, his right side was paralyzed, and the right side of his face drooped. At first he could not swallow. He was dreadfully spastic. And he would be wheelchair-dependent for the rest of his life.

Therapy in those days was rudimentary at best, but he did learn to speak again and was able to recover some use of his arms and legs. He also learned to swallow again.

When his parents took him home, his wife was gone. A couple of months later, he was served with divorce papers, and he never saw or heard from her again.

John's dad and uncle ran a furniture store, and for years John hung around there with them. When his dad and mother died, he still kept on with his uncle. Then the uncle died, and the store was sold. John was left alone. He was on his own. He moved into a nursing home for a while. Then the nursing home set up Columbia Place, and John was the first resident.

When Annie and I first began to help out at Columbia Place, we would see John from time to time, making his way around. He sat on the front edge of his wheelchair seat, leaning way back, and propelled himself by "walking" with his legs. He had a woman friend named Ruth who lived with him. It was a cooperative relationship, with her doing the cooking and cleaning and John providing the finances from the modest trust fund his parents and uncle had left him. He and Ruth had met at the nursing home and both were glad to be at Columbia Place.

Soon, Ruth was taken to the hospital and died within a few days. Ruth's sons had not told John anything about her condition, and did not even tell him when she died. He finally asked a friend to call the hospital and check on her. The friend ascertained that she had died several days earlier. John had missed the funeral. He was devastated over yet another loss and the painful rejection from Ruth's family.

When we met John, we knew nothing of his background. He was a gregarious, affable guy, and we had no idea what sorrow was accumulating in his heart. We invited him to the Bible study on Monday nights, and he started coming. He had a million questions. Those questions, and their answers, provided the basis for our study for a good long time. We learned about John's history—a rich history indeed. His dad, as a city councilman, was involved in some of the exciting early growth of Atlanta. He often took John along to meetings and social events, where John had met many of the most interesting people in Atlanta's past.

John wanted to know how a loving God could bring such a series of disasters to his life. We did, too. But there is no easy answer to that question. Although we tried for months, we finally decided that we just have to accept some things in faith and leave the answers to God. John finally decided he could do that, and he professed his love for Jesus and his trust in Him. Instead of, "Why me?" the question became, "Why not me?"

I was still selling in those days, and because he loved to travel, I took John along on a couple of day trips. He also loved to talk, and he never slowed down, no matter how many hours we rode. At the end of the day, I felt like I'd been shot at by a machine gun. But we both had a good time.

One night in Bible study at our house, John pulled up his shirt and showed us a large mole growing right in the middle of his chest. He said, "What about this?" A chill ran through my body. Even from across the room, I was sure it was a melanoma. I told him we were going to the VA that week.

The biopsy results were not good. The doctors wanted John to come back in for a more thorough surgical procedure. John was terrified. He asked Annie all kinds of questions. He just could not understand how they could put him to sleep and cut him without waking him up. Annie went through the entire process with him and assured him he would not feel a thing. She went to the hospital the morning of the surgery and she was there when they took John to the operating room.

When he came back, Annie heard his voice in the hall and went to him. John hollered out, "You were right, it was exactly like you said it would be." They had taken out more tissue from his chest and scraped the bone on his sternum and ribs. They put him on some chemotherapy and John went on with life. They did follow-up tests periodically, and it was no surprise a couple of years later when the cancer returned and had spread throughout John's body. We discussed the situation with him, and he decided he wanted to go home and be with his friends when he died.

After years of watching a terrible old television set, I finally convinced him to use a little of his "rainy day" money for a new one. He was thrilled that he could now see the pictures clearly.

I had done John's will, and was executor of his estate. I also officiated at his funeral. There were a couple of surprises. Two of John's cousins came to the funeral and told me how close they had been to John, how they had visited him many times. I had been around for eight years and had never seen anybody come to visit John. They asked about a will, and I told them there was one, but that they were not in it. They left. Then John's former wife showed up. She did not ask about the will. She said that she had been the one who had ordered the flowers and fruit baskets that John had found outside his door for many years. She said she stayed away because when she remarried, she married a man who had been John's best friend in high school. He had visited John many times, never telling John who he had married. She apologized for neglecting him.

We learned a lot from John. No matter how many

times he got knocked down, he always got up and kept going. He had a wonderful sense of humor and an incredible attitude. He had once been a very handsome man, but even though the stroke had left his face disfigured and his body nonfunctional, he kept going on. He showed us all how to be positive and confident under the worst of circumstances.

Another person we learned a lot from was a man named Hugh Harris. Hugh had been a lifelong smoker and had high blood pressure. At age fifty-three, he had a huge stroke. He lost the use of his right side and became aphasic. He could not get his voice to do what his mind was telling it. Before his stroke he had been an accountant in the chicken industry and his stay-at-home wife, Elizabeth, had always waited on him hand and foot. It was only natural that she continued after the stroke. They lived that way until, eleven years later, she died suddenly of a heart attack. Hugh was devastated. There was no way he could live alone. He tried living with his son in Atlanta for a few weeks, but that proved to be a disastrous situation. So he went to El Paso, Texas, and lived with his daughter.

Within a few weeks, his daughter had had enough. Unable to cope with her dad's disability and constant demands, she told him she was not going to wait on him anymore and that he had to learn to take care of himself. He learned to make a sandwich and fix his own lunch. But he was such an irascible old coot that his daughter finally bought him a ticket back to Atlanta. Rob found him an apartment at Columbia Place and unceremoniously dumped him there with a few furniture items to help make him comfortable. But he was miserable.

Enter Ed and Annie.

Fortunately, Hugh had come to terms with his attitude and decided he had better adjust to the reality of his life if he was going to survive living alone. We found him to be a rather pleasant gentleman. He became a regular in our group and our Monday night Bible study. Since he couldn't talk much, we didn't learn a great deal about him for a good while. But, inevitably, his story slowly emerged.

Hugh was very suspicious of us for a long time, but bit by bit he came to realize that we really were there because we wanted to help. He loved Bible study when he finally joined us and participated in the discussions. The rest of us waited patiently while he struggled to say what he wanted to—except for John, who would try to help Hugh by finishing his sentences or trying to guess what Hugh was trying to say. It made Hugh furious.

One night, Hugh got so mad at John that he scooted across the room with his cane raised over his head. Luckily, I was nimble and quick enough to prevent Hugh from whacking John over the head. John was not coordinated enough to defend himself. They could get along all right, as long as John didn't interrupt. We had tried to get John to quit that, but it took this incident to finally shut him up.

Hugh was a quieter traveling companion than John, and I took him on several of my selling trips, even some overnights. Hugh loved movies, particularly science fiction, so on overnight trips we went to the movies together. We were in Dothan, Alabama, one time and he talked me into going to a movie called *The Last Starfighter.* I loved it and it has become one of my all-time favorites. I have it on both videotape and DVD.

On one of our trips together, Hugh told me he had one regret about his life. He had never told his daughter Mary Beth that he loved her. I was shocked. He said he couldn't say it over the phone, and she couldn't afford to come for a visit. I tracked her down and called her. I told her that Hugh desperately wanted to talk to her, and that I would pay her way to fly to Georgia.

She told me she would rather drive her car so she could bring her daughter, so I told her I would buy the gas and pay for the motel rooms coming and going. They would stay with Annie and me. A couple of weeks later, she called to say she was on the way and would be here the next day. That was when I told Hugh she was coming.

The next morning I went early to fetch him. I sat Mary Beth directly in front of Hugh's wheelchair. They just stared at each other for a good while. Then I said softly, "Hugh, don't you have something you wanted to tell Mary Beth?"

There was a long pause while he struggled to produce the words. Then he suddenly blurted out, "I love you!"

Mary Beth sat stunned for a moment, then lunged and hugged her dad. When she quit sobbing, she said, "I have waited all my life to hear you say that. Why did you never tell me that before?"

Hugh struggled to answer and finally said, "I wanted to. I wanted to. I wanted to. I just couldn't. I'm sorry. So sorry. So sorry."

She moved closer to Hugh and took his good hand. She leaned forward and placed his hand on her cheek. "I love you, too, Daddy. I love you, too."

I left the room and let them share their feelings for as long as they wanted. When we went to lunch, they continued their sharing. Then we went back to the house, and they talked until Hugh said that he had to go home.

They spent the next three days together. They visited Rob, and then Rome, Taylorsville, and Cedartown. They visited relatives and saw Elizabeth's grave. Each night Mary Beth reported to me what they had done and thanked me for making it happen. When she finally had to leave, she told me Hugh had told her he loved her over and over again during those days. She refused my offer to help pay for the trip—and she said it was the best investment she had ever made. They hugged both of us and drove away. It had been a wonderful time for us, too, and it had a magical effect on Hugh. He was no longer the grumpy old man he had once been.

Soon after that visit, Hugh developed leukemia and began to require periodic blood transfusions. At first it was every couple of months, then monthly, then twice a month, then weekly. I took him to every session. I knew that his days were numbered by his willingness to continue the needle sticks and transfusions. The nurses at the DeKalb Medical Center transfusion center were wonderful, and Hugh became one of their favorites.

He had an enormously concerned doctor who, at one point, put Hugh into the hospital for a complete evaluation, telling me that Hugh was about to run out of options. I contacted Hugh's son, who had visited his dad frequently. Hugh finally told me that he didn't want any more transfusions. He had already had more than one hundred. He repeated over and over, "No more, no more, no more."

I called the nurse, requesting a visit from Hugh's doctor. As we waited, Hugh and I talked about all the fun we had had together, and he reminded me about seeing *The Last Starfighter*. We had a wonderful time reminiscing.

When the doctor got there, he went over the medical implications of Hugh's decision. Hugh let him know he fully understood that without another transfusion, he could live only a few days. He repeated, "Ready to go, ready to go, ready to go, ready to go." His mind was made up.

The next morning, when Annie and I got to his room he said, "Elizabeth," and pointed to a corner of the room. I said, "Are you telling me Elizabeth is over there?" He nodded emphatically. I said, "She has come for you, Hugh."

"Yeah," he answered, then repeated, "Ready to go, ready to go, ready to go." I had talked to Rob the previous night, and he told me he was coming that afternoon. Annie and I left just before noon. It was clear that Hugh was fading.

At dusk, a nurse called to tell us that Hugh had just died. Rob had been there and left about thirty minutes earlier. We told her we were on our way. Hugh looked more peaceful than we had seen him since Mary Beth had left four years earlier. The nurse told us that Hugh had called her into his room and motioned for her to sit beside him on the bed. She did, and put her arm over Hugh's shoulders.

He was breathing short, gasping breaths, which she recognized as his final ones. Then he suddenly sat up, looked straight into the corner of the room and almost shouted, "Elizabeth!" Then a big smile spread over his face and he lay back on the bed and took his final breath.

Hugh had chosen the time and place for his death and had been greeted by the one true love of his life. What a way to go.

Rob was executor of his estate, and I presided at his funeral. We drove Hugh's body the seventy miles to Cedartown, where he and Elizabeth had lived. Some relatives gathered at the cemetery and we had a commitment service, laying him beside his beloved Elizabeth. Hugh was home.

------------ TERESA, CHRIS, AND RITA ------------

Early in our ministry, we had taken a group of our friends to South DeKalb Mall. As we were loading up to take them home, a woman asked me if we were a transportation service for people in wheelchairs. I told her about our ministry and she asked me what it cost to make a trip. I told her it was all absolutely free. She told me she had a friend with multiple sclerosis who lived in her apartment building and needed rides to different places. I gave her a card and told her to have her friend call me.

A few days later, I had a call from a woman whose Bronx accent immediately enchanted me. She told me about her life with MS, and asked if I could take her to the dentist the following week. I affirmed that appointment— and you would have thought I had promised her a ride to heaven. She told me she had a developmentally disabled brother and sister who would go along, but that they did not require much supervision.

When I arrived for the pick-up, they were waiting outside the building. I finally understood her name as Teresa Rienzie. She introduced her brother and sister as Chris and Rita. They mumbled a response, and then Teresa told me that the two of them had a language all their own and did not talk much in plain English. I had heard of that phenomenon before. Though they couldn't read, write, or tell time, they actually communicated extremely well between themselves.

When we got to the dental office, I pushed Teresa into the waiting room. Chris and Rita sat next to her, and I sat across the room. When the dental tech pushed her out of the waiting room, Chris and Rita immediately got up and sat next to me. I was reading a magazine. They mimicked my movements, thumbing through the pages, looking at the pictures.

The moment Teresa came out of the back, they both moved to her. Chris took the push handles of her chair and Rita stood beside her. They were protecting her.

Teresa told me they were from a family of twelve children. Chris and Rita were the youngest. There was another sister, Mary, who lived in Augusta, Georgia. She was available when they needed her. Teresa was my age and was an Air Force veteran. Chris and Rita were two and four years younger.

I took them many places over the years. We went to doctors, dentists, drug stores, and grocery stores. I came to have a profound respect for all of them. This was an amazing relationship. Teresa needed someone to help her with her physical needs as MS slowly destroyed her body. Chris and Rita needed someone to help with their mental needs. It was a perfect synergistic relationship. Teresa would sit in the doorway of the kitchen and instruct Chris and Rita as they prepared the meals. They got Teresa out of bed every morning, gave her a shower, brushed her teeth, dressed her, and put her in her electric recliner. They did all the laundry and cleaned the house. Teresa had a schedule for every task and supervised every step.

Chris and Rita always called me Santa Claus, and a couple of times I wore my full red suit out to their house. I took each of them a cuddly stuffed teddy bear. They loved it.

They bought a house and lived together until the MS

ran its course and Teresa died. Mary told me that when she shared the news with Chris and Rita, they stood and stared at her for a few minutes. Then Chris said, "Well, that is over." The two of them sat down on the couch to watch TV. They did not mention Teresa again. There was no service. She was cremated, and her ashes were to be scattered when they went back to New York someday.

It was an amazing story of how family members should stick together and take care of each other. That doesn't always happen. In this case it did happen, in an amazing way.

final *miracles*

When the sums of all these "little" miracles are added up, it amounts to some bigger, rather significant ones.

We began FODAC in my garage, and now we are in a 64,885-square-foot building. It was quite a process that got us here, but seeing it is still a shock for all of us at FODAC and for our visitors. Every time I pull into the parking lot, I still can't believe all this has happened to us.

Inside, the 40,000-square-foot warehouse is crammed with medical equipment of all kinds, shapes, sizes, and descriptions. We have thousands of parts and hundreds of devices. There are shelves and pallet racks everywhere. The parts themselves are worth millions of dollars. They haven't cost FODAC a single cent. The offices and shop spaces are filled with desks, computers, chairs, and artwork on the walls. Some spaces even have fancy lighting. And it all came to us as donations. We have a sixteen-foot-long conference table in our boardroom.

A donation. I can't walk through our building without thinking all the time, "What an awesome God we serve."

Consider the effects that all these miracles have had. We gave away our ten thousandth wheelchair in December of 2003. We are probably over 17,000 by now, in March of 2007. We just haven't stopped to count them all. We have provided wheelchairs to people in forty-two states and in sixty-eight countries. Those numbers are mind-boggling. We started out to help the twelve people we were already connected to, and now over 60,000 people have benefited from our obedience to our loving Lord.

We have an area in our office spaces where we have put thank-you notes up on the wall. There are hundreds of them. Any time the staff or I need a boost, we can re-charge our batteries by reading some of these letters. Just walking by them gives me all the charge I need.

Our ramps program has built over 700 ramps all over north Georgia. Every one of them represents an entire family whose lives are made just a little bit easier. People are able to go to church, to the store, and to medical appointments again with minimal assistance.

Hundreds more people have found affordable clothing in our thrift store. We have given clothing and furniture to families who have lost their homes. We've given clothing to homeless people who are going on job interviews. To shelters, we have given refrigerators and freezers and mattresses—literally, tons of them.

We've been able to provide people with vehicles. We have enabled several people with disabilities to go to college. We have made it possible for families that have been completely homebound to get out and enjoy life again. Is it any wonder that people call me Santa Claus?

It has been a remarkable adventure, this trip. We have never once doubted that we were doing the exact thing that God wanted us to do. Of course there has been some anxiety from time to time, when things didn't happen when or how we thought they should. But we have come to realize that God's timetable is different from ours. He has come through on His schedule, which usually works out better than ours would have anyway.

I found out at the age of fifty that He was waiting for me to yield to Him, and then He went right to work making things happen. Our God is a gentleman; He never forces Himself on anyone. He is available to you, too. If you haven't already, why don't you invite Him to take control of your life, and find out what special joy He can bring to your heart?

That good feeling doesn't require a red suit and a white beard. It does require wearing Christ's love right out there where people can see and feel it. It does require being kind and loving in all your dealings with everyone. Yes, even with clerks in stores, tellers at the bank, service writers at the auto repair shop, and everyone else you encounter. Put a smile on your face and see how many more smiles you see in return. It is contagious—pass it around! Jesus gave us two commands: love God and love your neighbors. It's simple, really. Show your love for God by loving your neighbors. Find a way to do that. Reach out to others in love. Volunteer at a service charity. Build a Habitat house. Give blood. Mow your neighbor's lawn. Be the type of person you'd like to be.

Be somebody's Santa Claus.

## ED BUTCHART—REAL LIFE SANTA

-------------------------------------------------------------------------

IN ADDITION TO HIS MANY OTHER PUBLIC AND PRIVATE APPEARANCES AS SANTA, ED BUTCHART HAD BEEN THE OFFICIAL SANTA AT GEORGIA'S STONE MOUNTAIN PARK FOR 17 YEARS. HE IS ALSO THE FOUNDER AND EXECUTIVE DIRECTOR EMERITUS OF FODAC, FRIENDS OF DISABLED ADULTS AND CHILDREN, REPAIRING WHEELCHAIRS AND OTHER MEDICAL EQUIPMENT FOR PEOPLE WHO OTHERWISE COULD NOT AFFORD SUCH LIFE-CHANGING BENEFITS. HIS PUBLIC SERVICE AND PERSONAL WORK HAVE BROUGHT MR. BUTCHART, WHO LIVES IN GREENVILLE, SOUTH CAROLINA, MANY HUMANITARIAN AWARDS. FOR MORE INFORMATION, VISIT THE WEB SITE: WWW.REALTHINGSANTA.COM.

# The EASTER STORY

## For Children

Ralph W. Sockman
Illustrated by
Gordon Laite

ABINGDON PRESS
new york       nashville

To all the grandchildren
I have been told about
and
To the Four I like to
talk about

The greatest birthday of all time and in all the world is celebrated on Christmas Day.

We like to have big times on our own birthdays. Sometimes we have cakes with candles on them. Others know how old we are by the number of candles on our birthday cakes. Often somebody gives us a present. We receive cards with jolly good wishes. Birthdays are happy times because those who love us are glad that we are alive.

The greatest birthday is Christmas. Why? It is the birthday of the best man that ever lived. His name was Jesus. He was born many, many years ago in the little town of Bethlehem.

Every Christmas we hear the story of how Jesus was born in a manger because there was no room for Mary, his mother, in the inn. It seems too bad that Jesus had to be born in a stable and not in a nice house or hospital. We do not cry about it for

that little manger was made a happy,
beautiful place by the love of those
gathered around it. Shepherds came
singing songs of gladness. Wise men
brought gifts. Mary's heart was filled
with love and joy as she held her first-
born baby in her arms.

When we celebrate Jesus' birthday we sing carols and say, "Merry Christmas," and we give presents.

Jesus was God's best gift to us. All of us are happier because he came.

Jesus worked and played as other boys did in the town of Nazareth where Mary and Joseph lived. He grew up to be a strong man. He was a carpenter. Maybe he helped to make carts and yokes for oxen. Maybe he built houses.

Most of the people around Jesus, the people who lived in Nazareth, were very poor.

They worked hard, but they could earn only a little money and they could not save. Cruel officials took away their money to pay taxes to those who ruled over them. When the people were sick, they had no good doctors to look after them.

They were like sheep without a shepherd to care for them.

Often Jesus watched the shepherds in the fields around Nazareth. He saw how they led the sheep into the shelters when storms came. Jesus saw shepherds carrying the little lambs that could not keep up with the others.

And Jesus felt that God was calling him to be a good shepherd. He would take care of the suffering people around him as the shepherds looked after their lambs.

So Jesus left his carpenter shop to go forth as the Good Shepherd of the people. Great flocks of people followed him. Little children ran to him. He took them up in his arms and told them stories. Sick people were brought to him.

Sometimes children helped him in his work. Once Jesus was talking to a great crowd of people. They listened quietly, and Jesus talked for a long time. Suddenly he realized they must be very hungry but they had brought nothing with them to eat.

There was one boy in the crowd who
had five loaves of bread and two fish.
Jesus asked the boy to bring these to
him. When he had thanked God for
the loaves and the fish, Jesus divided
the food among the people, and there
was more than enough for all.

Jesus did so many wonderful things and said so many wise words that the people wanted to make him king. They thought he would gather an army about him and drive the enemy out of their country. Jesus refused to be that kind of king because he did not believe in fighting with weapons that kill men.

This disappointed some of the people and they turned away from him. There were some who did not like him because he would not be the kind of king they wanted.

Others turned against him because he was good. Sometimes when a person is very good it makes those around him see how bad they are.

The enemies of Jesus wanted to get rid of him. They began to plan how they could kill him. They plotted with one of Jesus' followers, a man named Judas. Judas had turned against Jesus. One night when Jesus was out in a dark garden, Judas led some soldiers to him and Jesus was arrested.

The soldiers were rough. They made

a crown of thorns and put it on Jesus' head. Think of it! Jesus, who might have been king with a crown of gold, was led through the streets wearing a crown of thorns.

The thorns made his head bleed. The soldiers took him before a ruler named Pilate. Jesus was condemned to die.

The most cruel way of putting people to death was to nail them to a cross. The kind and loving Jesus was to die on a cross.

But he did not lose his courage or his love. He did not whimper. He saw

his mother standing nearby, and he said some loving words to her. He prayed God to forgive the men who were to kill him. He died talking to God, his father, as a son coming home.

When the crowd had gone away, some friends buried Jesus in a tomb.

Three days later something very exciting happened. In the early morning before the sun was up, a few of Jesus' friends went out to the place where he had been buried so that they might put sweet perfume on his body. As they walked along, they wondered how they would be able to roll away the big stone which blocked the door to Jesus' tomb. When they got there, they found the stone had been rolled away. One of the friends, whose name was Mary, ran to the city to tell other friends. They came back with her. The tomb was empty!

As Mary stood in the garden outside the tomb, she heard a voice saying, "Why are you crying?" Mary thought it was the gardener speaking. She did not look up but she answered, "Because they have taken away my Lord, and I know not where they have taken him." Then the voice said to her, "Mary." And at that, Mary's heart leaped, for she recognized Jesus' voice.

These things happened early on the morning of the day which we now call Easter. That same evening two more of Jesus' friends were walking along the road, leaving the city of Jerusalem.

The friends were lonesome and very discouraged, for they thought Jesus would never be with them again.

As they walked and talked, with their eyes on the ground, a stranger spoke to them, asking why they were so sad. And suddenly they recognized the speaker as Jesus.

By these and other signs the followers of Jesus were made to feel sure that he was still alive. He was the victor over death!

He is alive forever. Easter is the day of victory, the day of joy and gladness.

Not many years ago a boy was riding a horse home from school. It was late in the afternoon and the skies were growing dark. At a certain point a bridge was being repaired, and the boy had to ride his horse directly across the stream. It had been raining and the stream had risen. In the darkness the horse did not want to rush into the muddy water. As the boy tried to urge the horse on, a door opened in a farmhouse on the other side of the stream. Through the open door a lamp cast a path of light. In the beam of light the horse and the boy gained new courage and were able to cross the stream with confidence.

Sometimes death is described as crossing a stream from this world into the next. The wisest men in all ages have believed there is a life beyond the grave. When Jesus rose from the tomb on Easter morning, he made a path of light which takes away our fear of death. Death is not going down into darkness but up into light.

We decorate our homes and churches at Easter because life is meant to be beautiful. Sometimes in our homes we have Easter eggs. An egg reminds us that life is being renewed always. Somehow in an eggshell a live chick or a baby bird is formed. One day the chick pecks its way through the shell and peeks out. Its eyes are filled with surprise and wonder. And why not? What a fine world this must seem to that fuzzy-headed little chick.

Flowers, too, show us that life is always coming back. During the winter

the earth looks dead, except down in the sunny southland where it doesn't get very cold. In other parts of our country the grass disappears in winter. The trees lose their leaves. But when spring comes the grass returns, new leaves appear on the trees, and flowers lift their lovely heads. This good earth has life which the cold cannot kill.

Life is always coming back to the earth in many different ways. The glory of Easter was revealed to us nearly two thousand years ago. The cross on which Jesus died has become a thing of beauty which we wear and put in our churches.

When Jesus came back to comfort

his friends they then knew, as we know, that life goes on and on and on.

As the cross became a thing of beauty, so Easter became the proof that God keeps his promises to his children. His love is with us always.